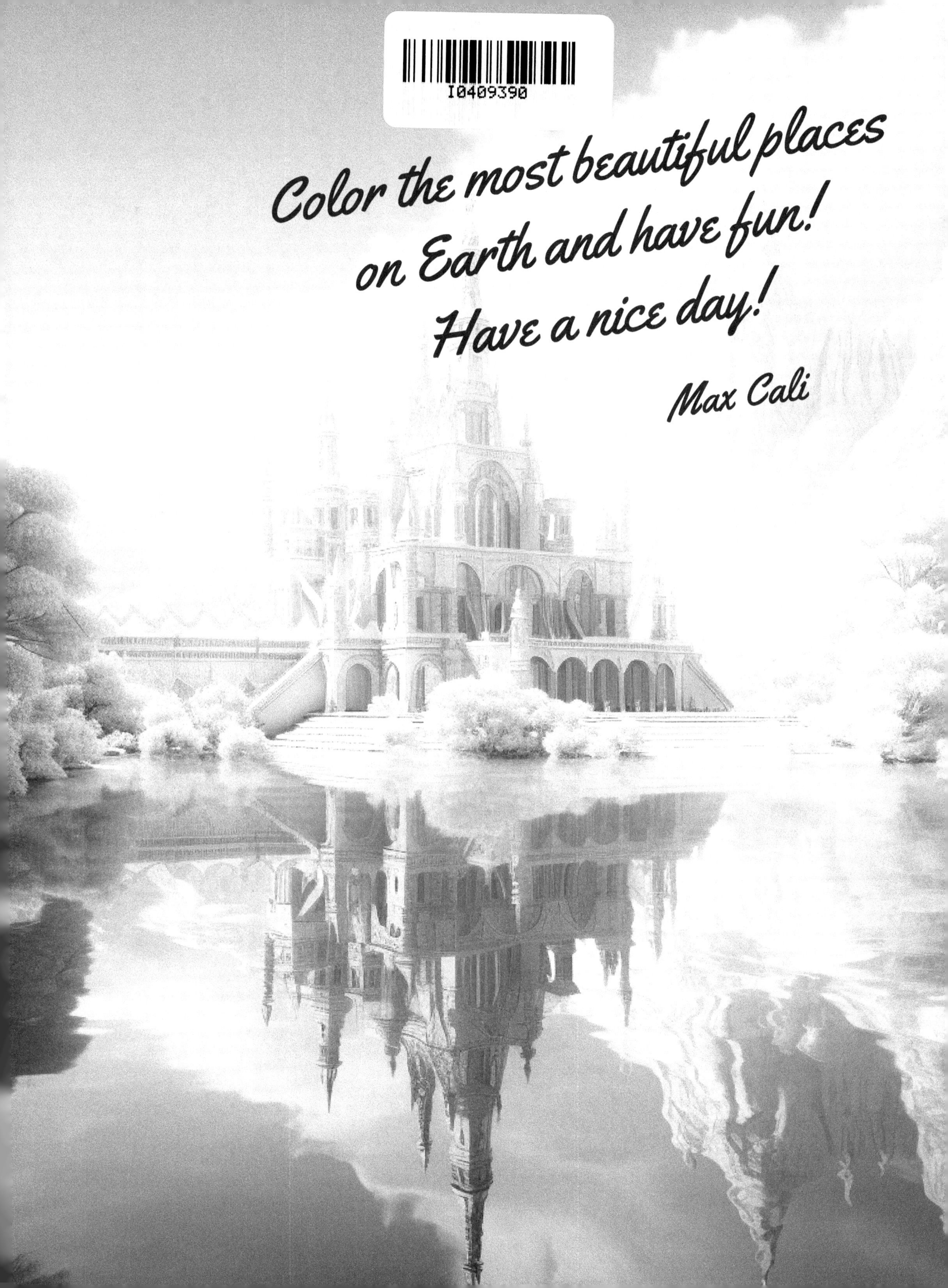

Color the most beautiful places
on Earth and have fun!
Have a nice day!

Max Cali

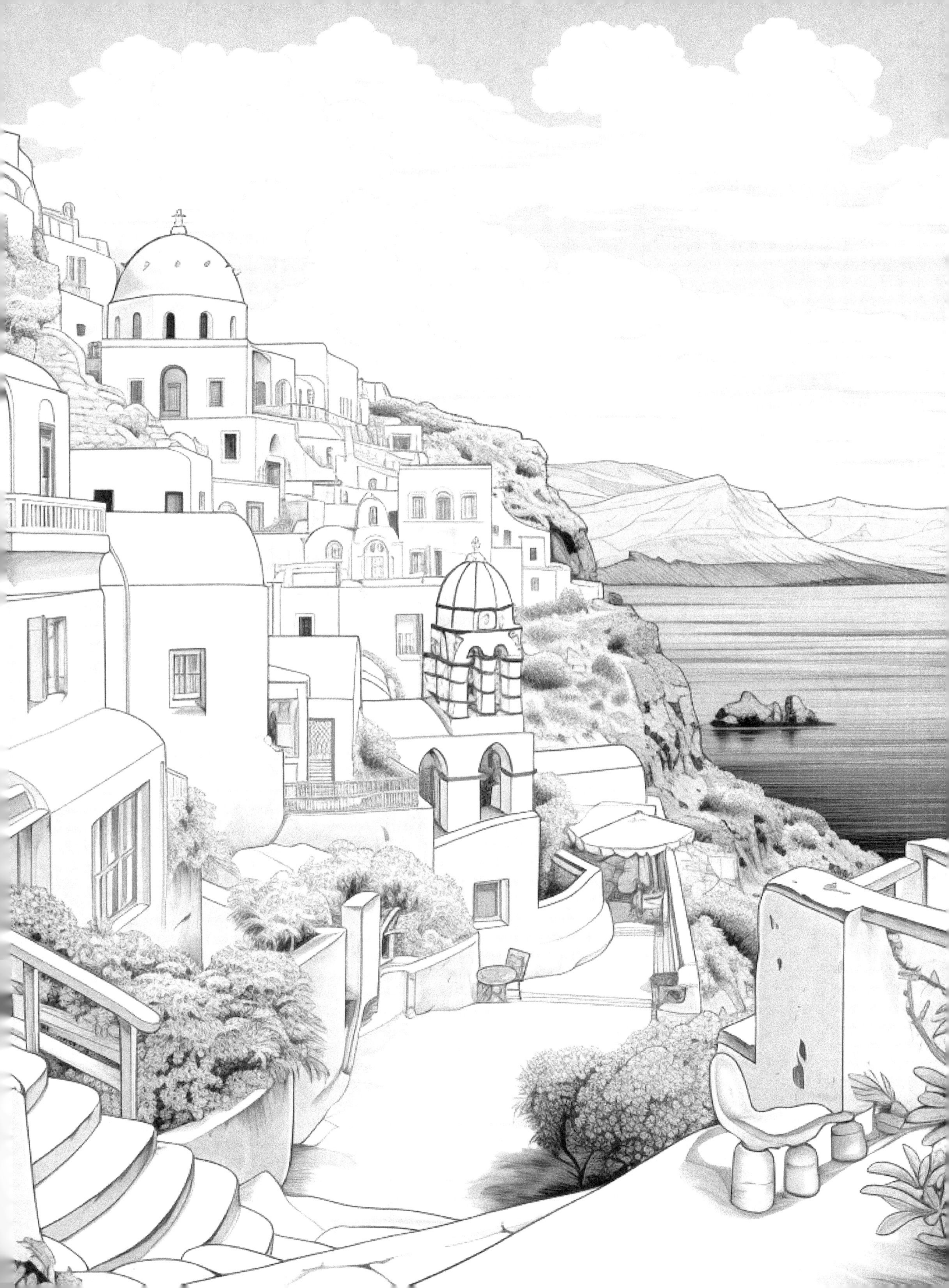

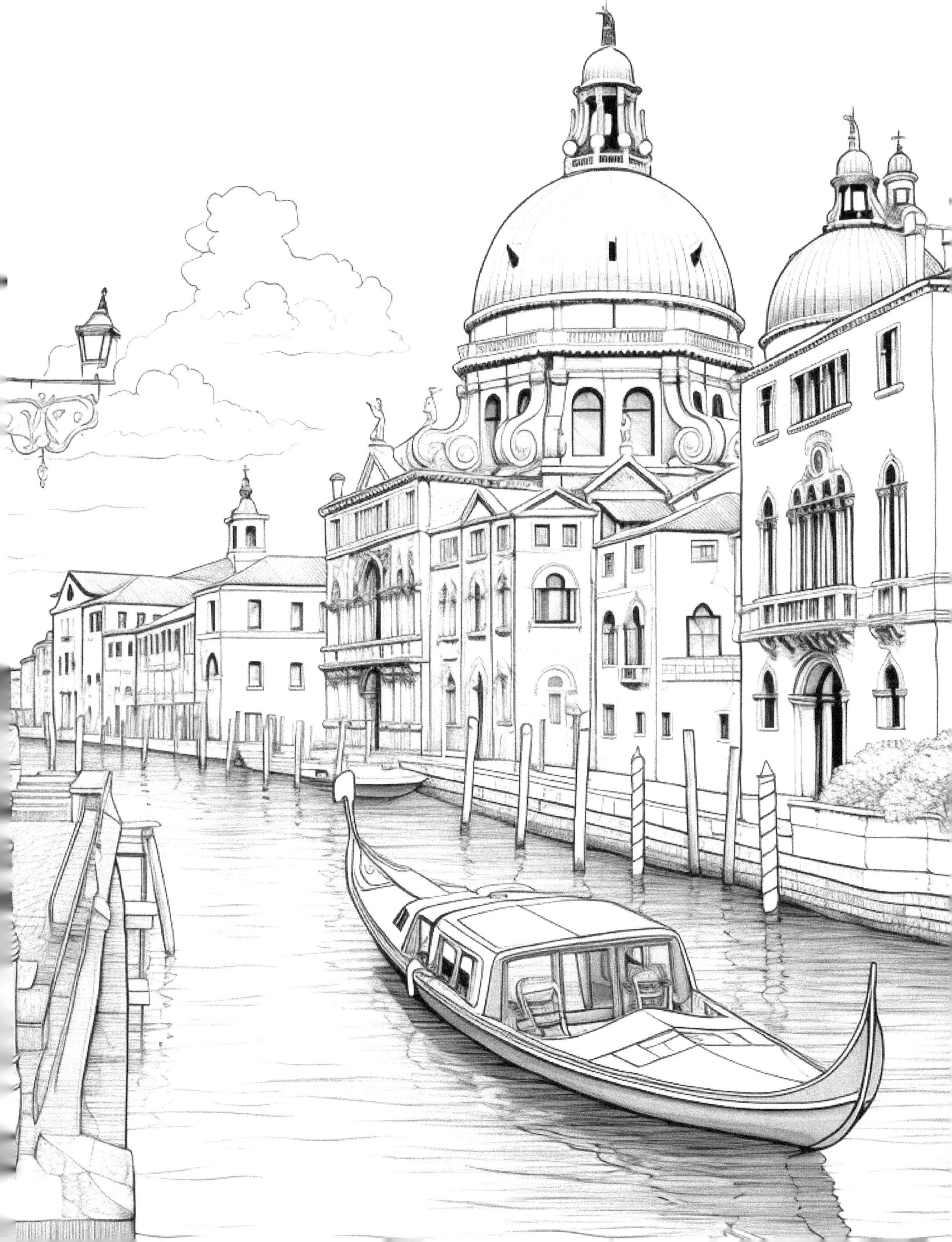

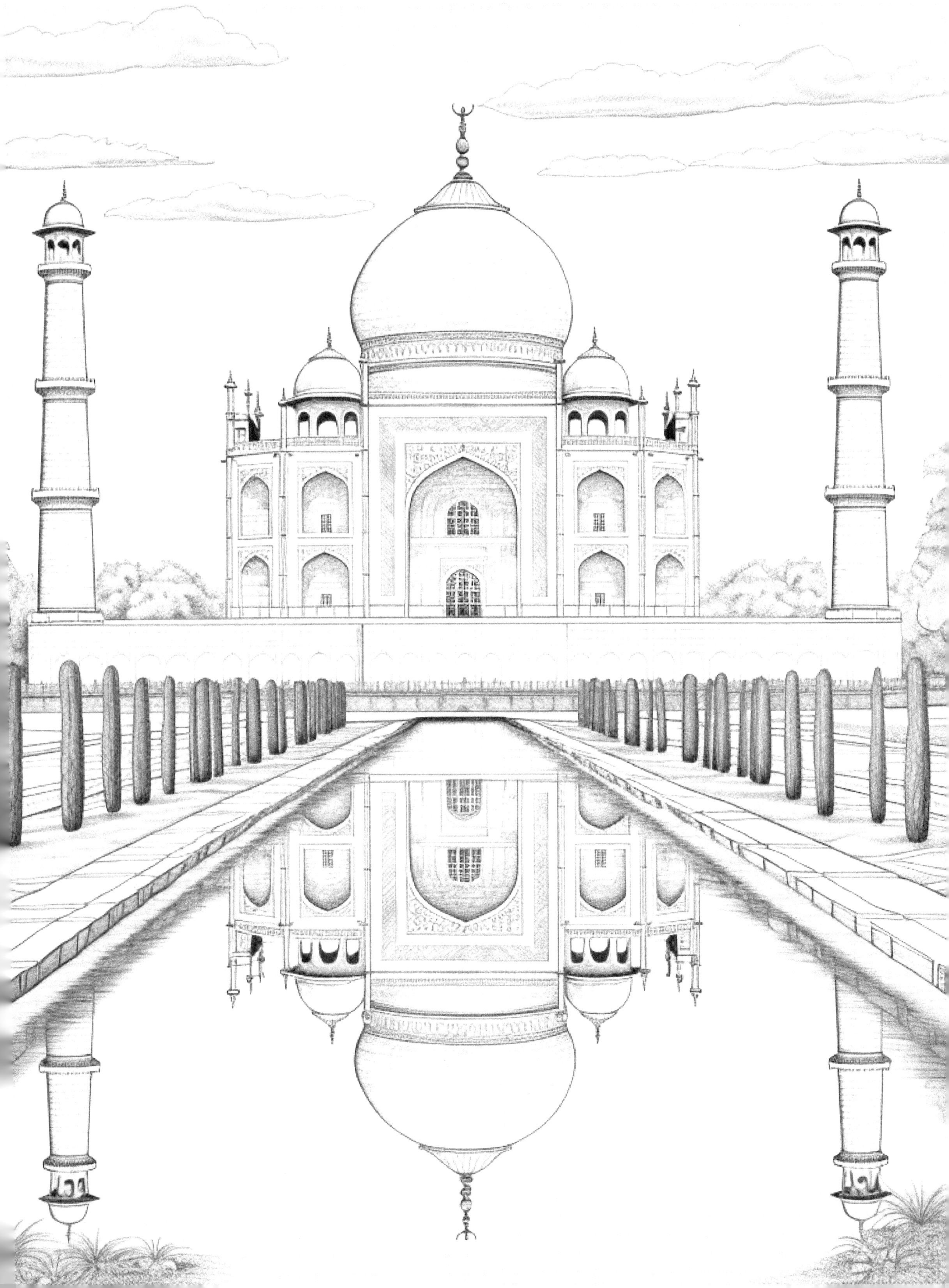

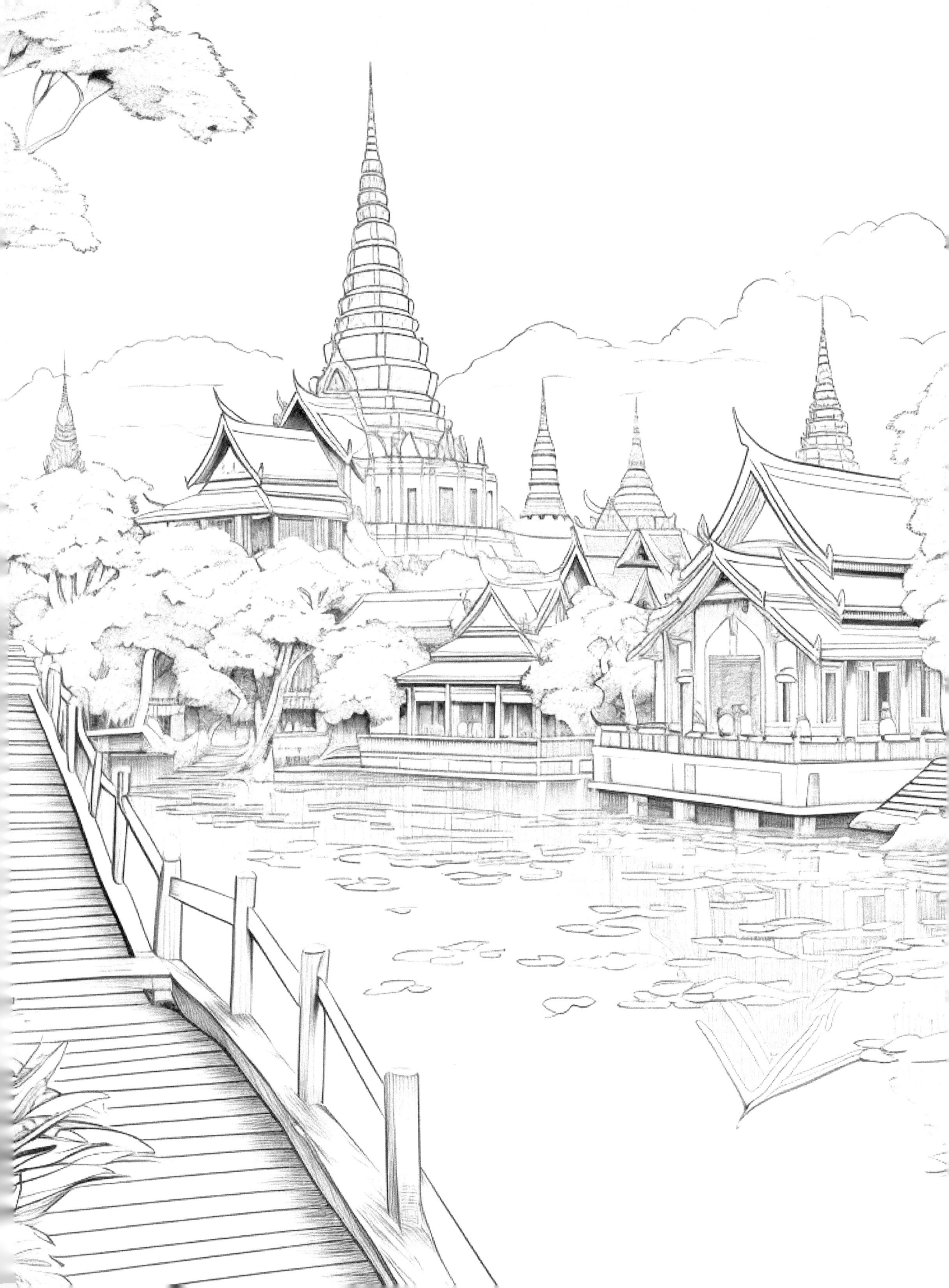

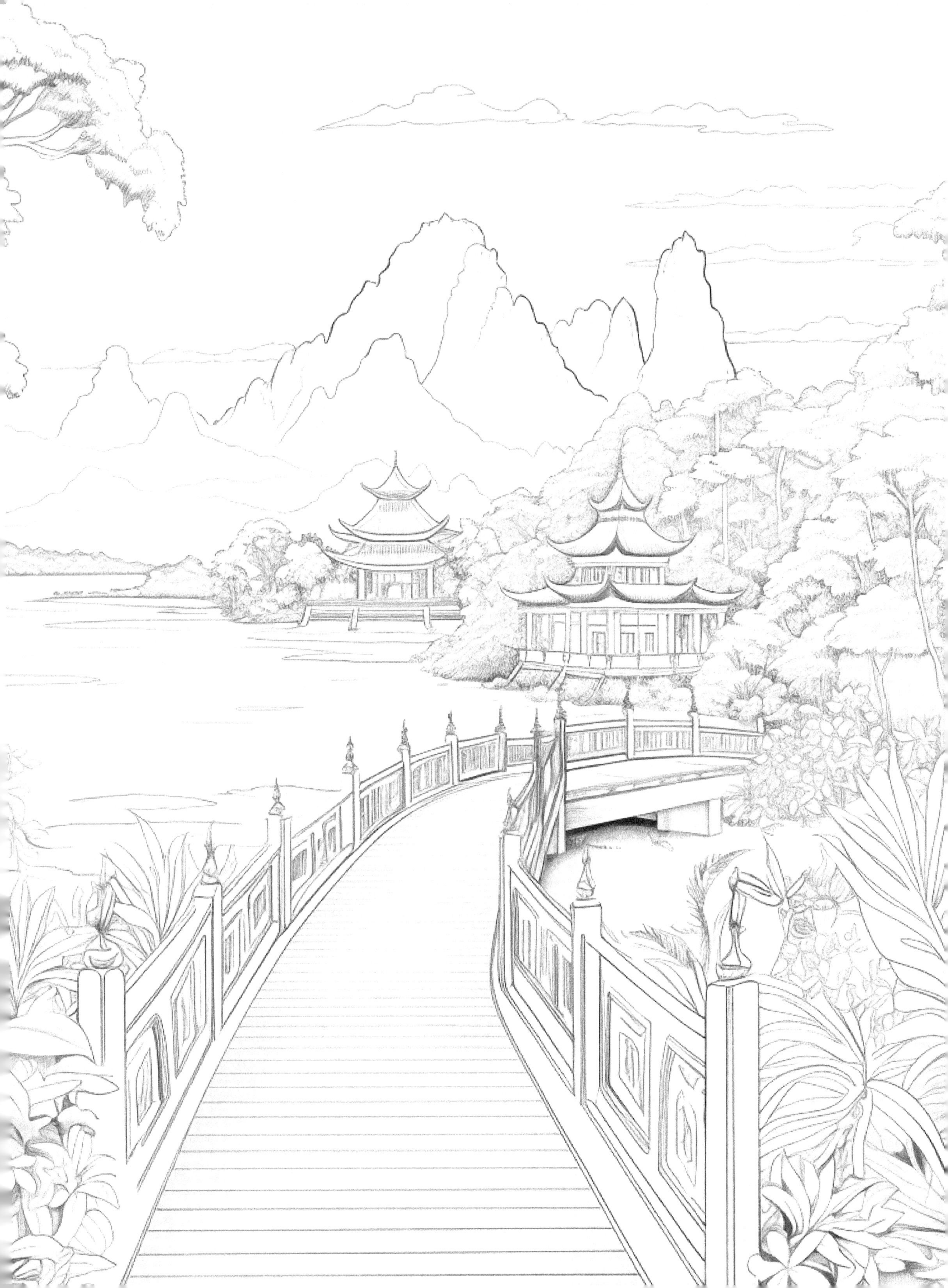

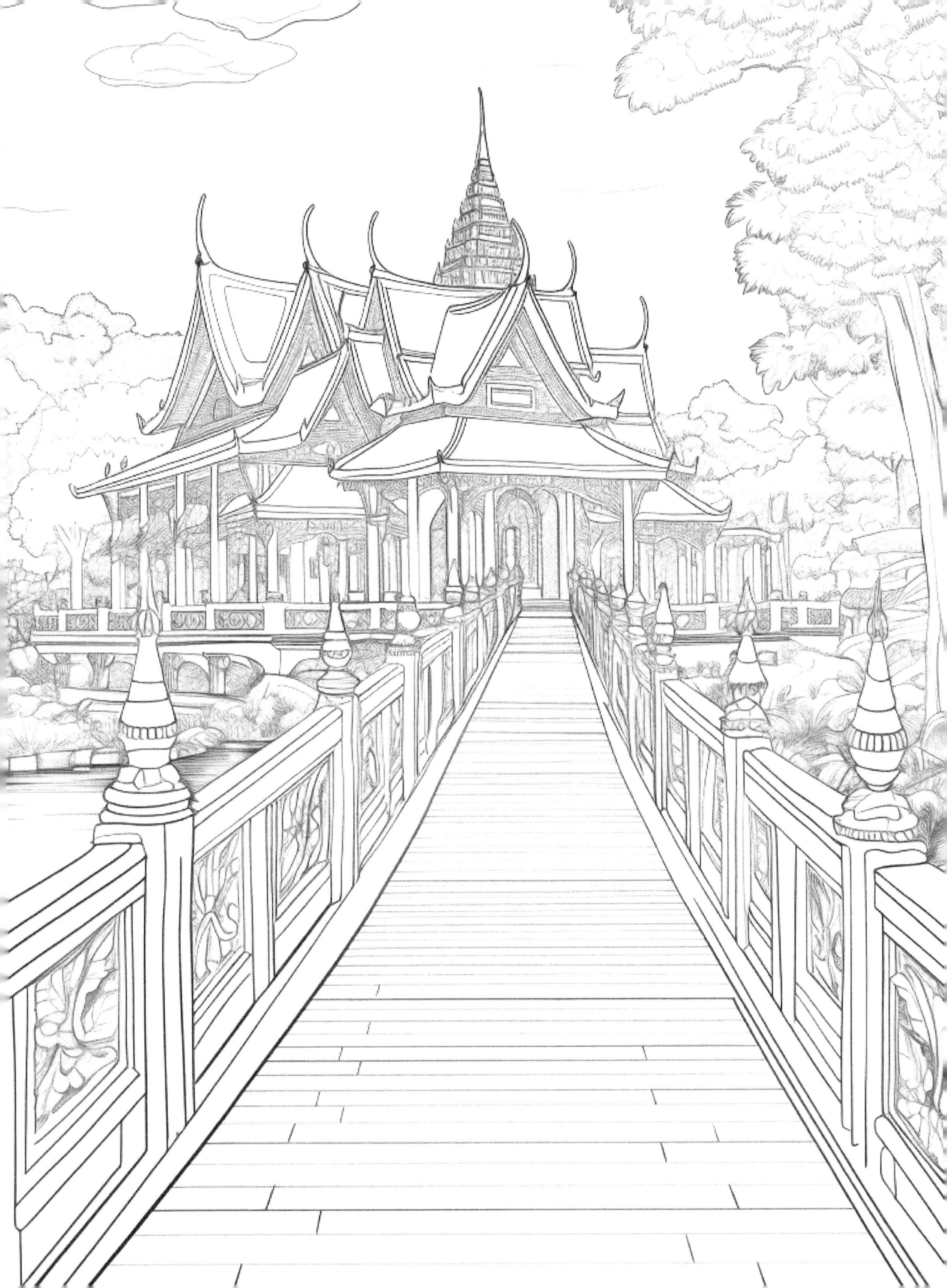

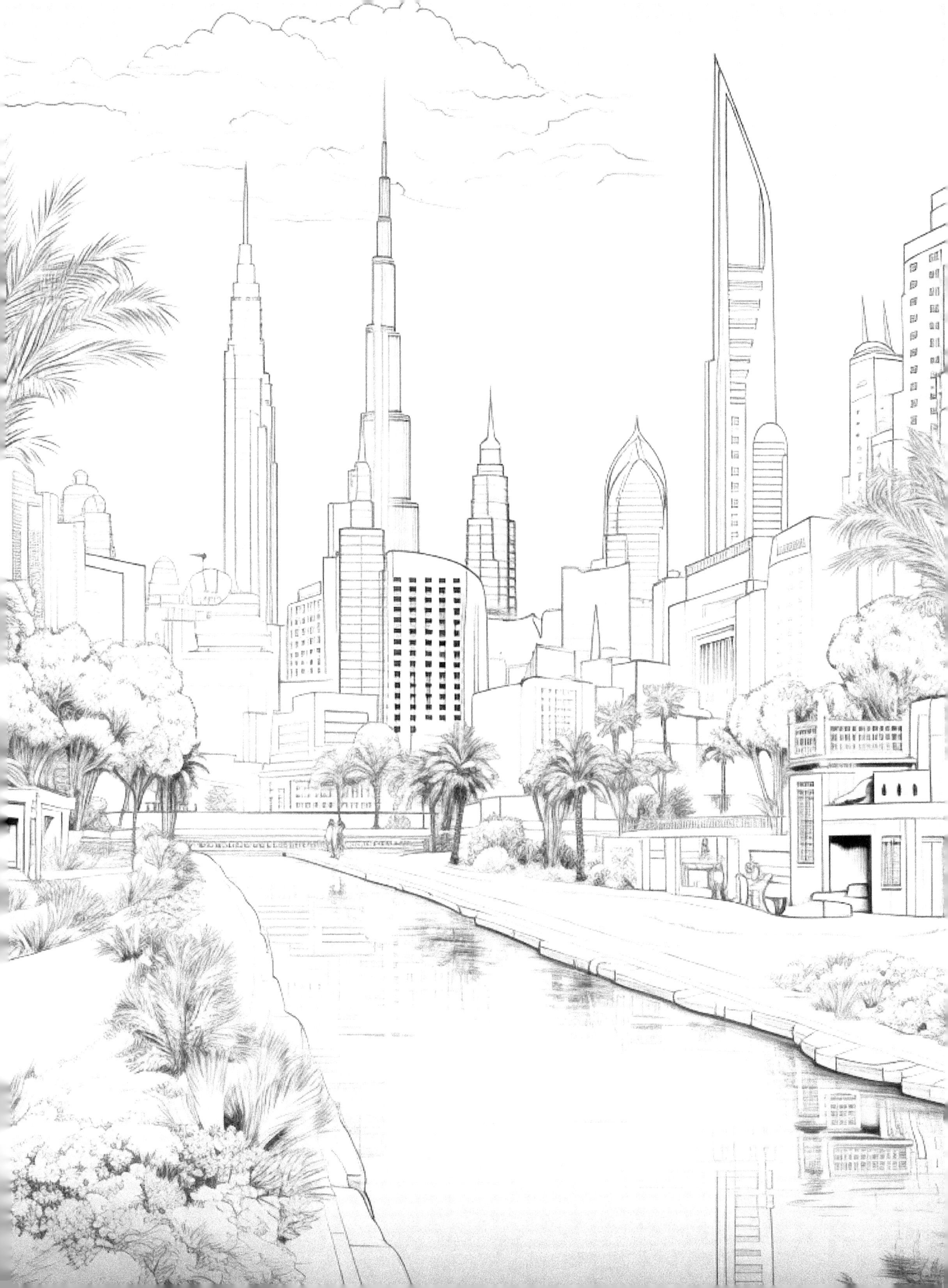

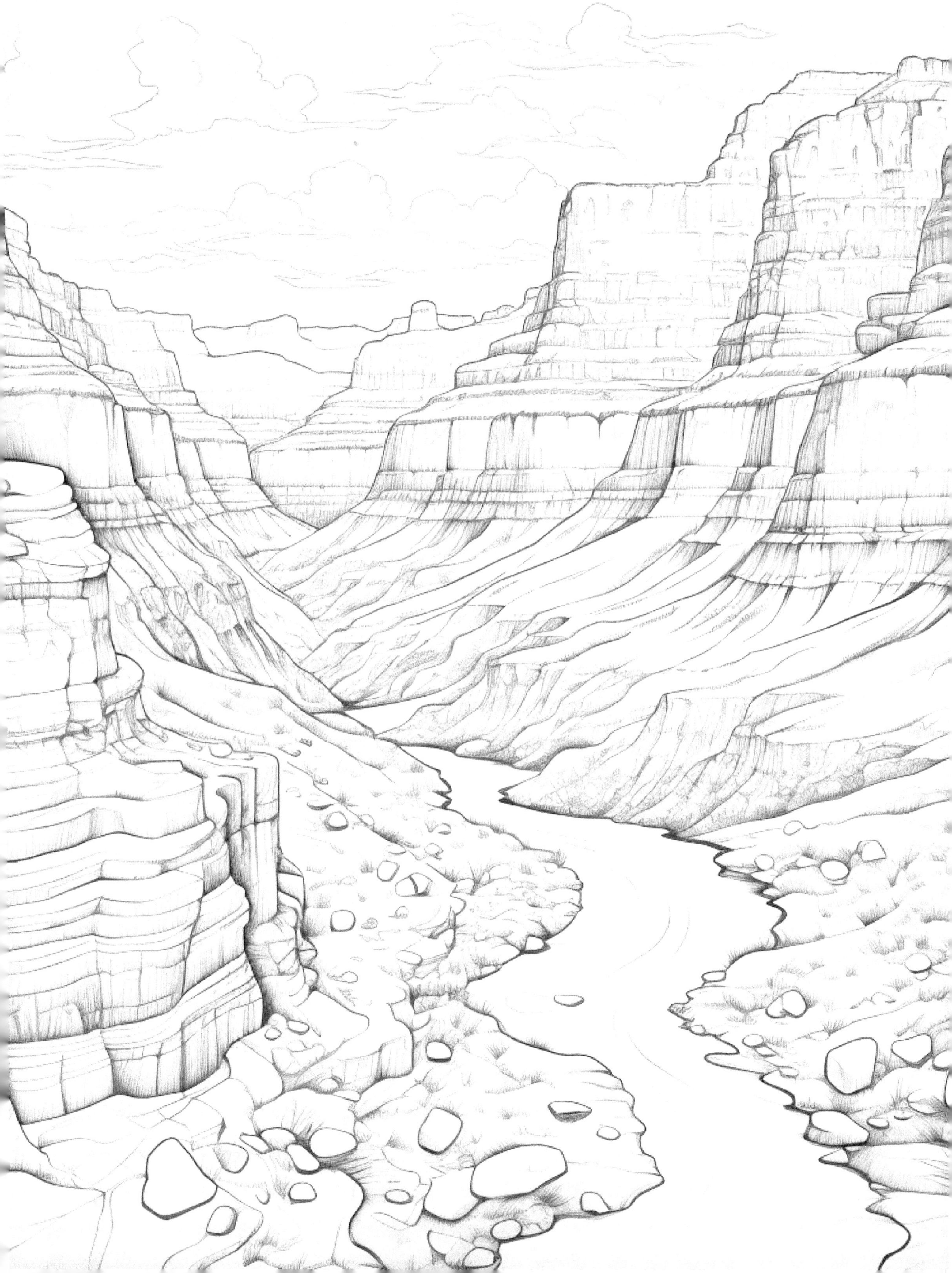

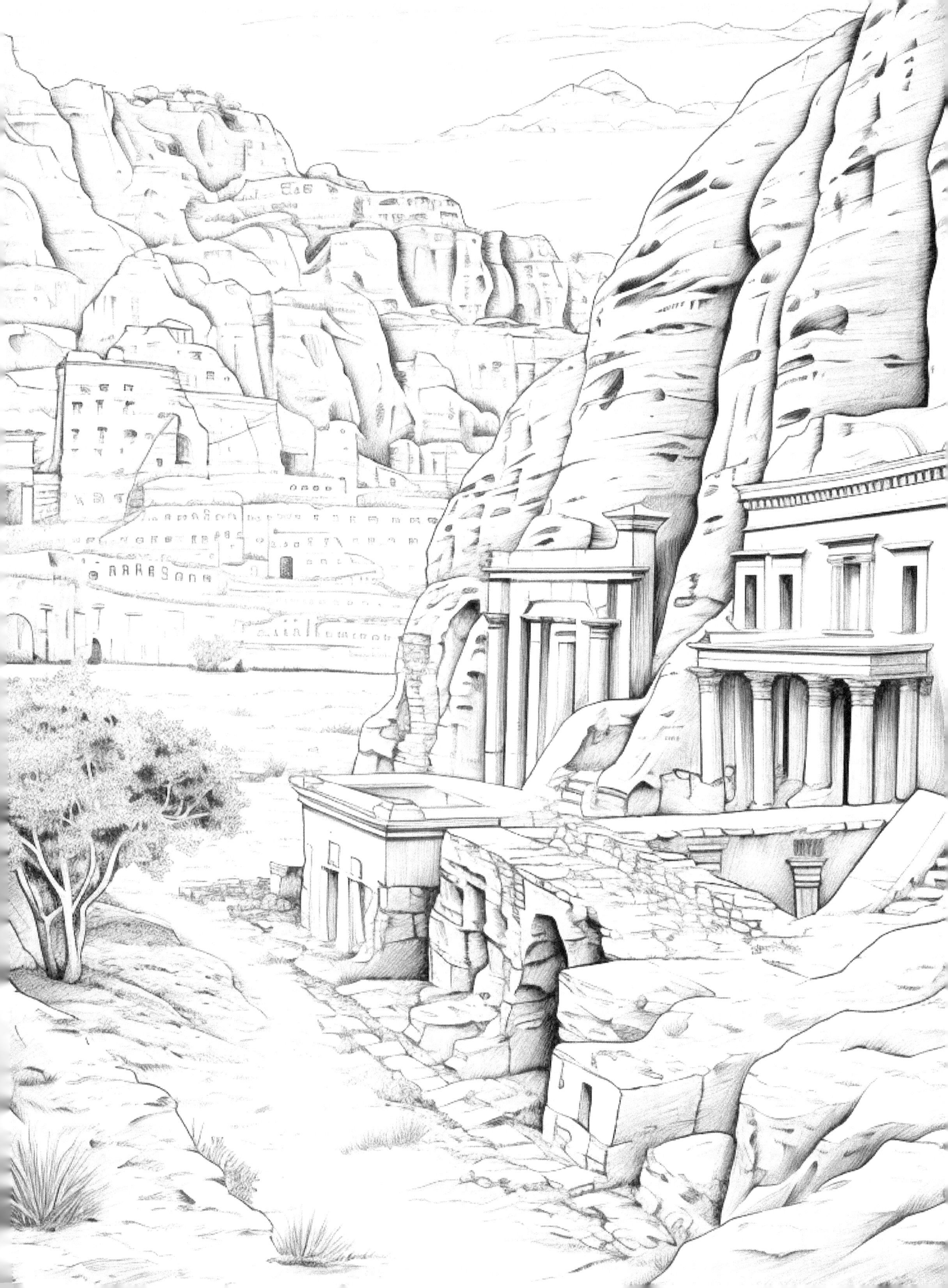

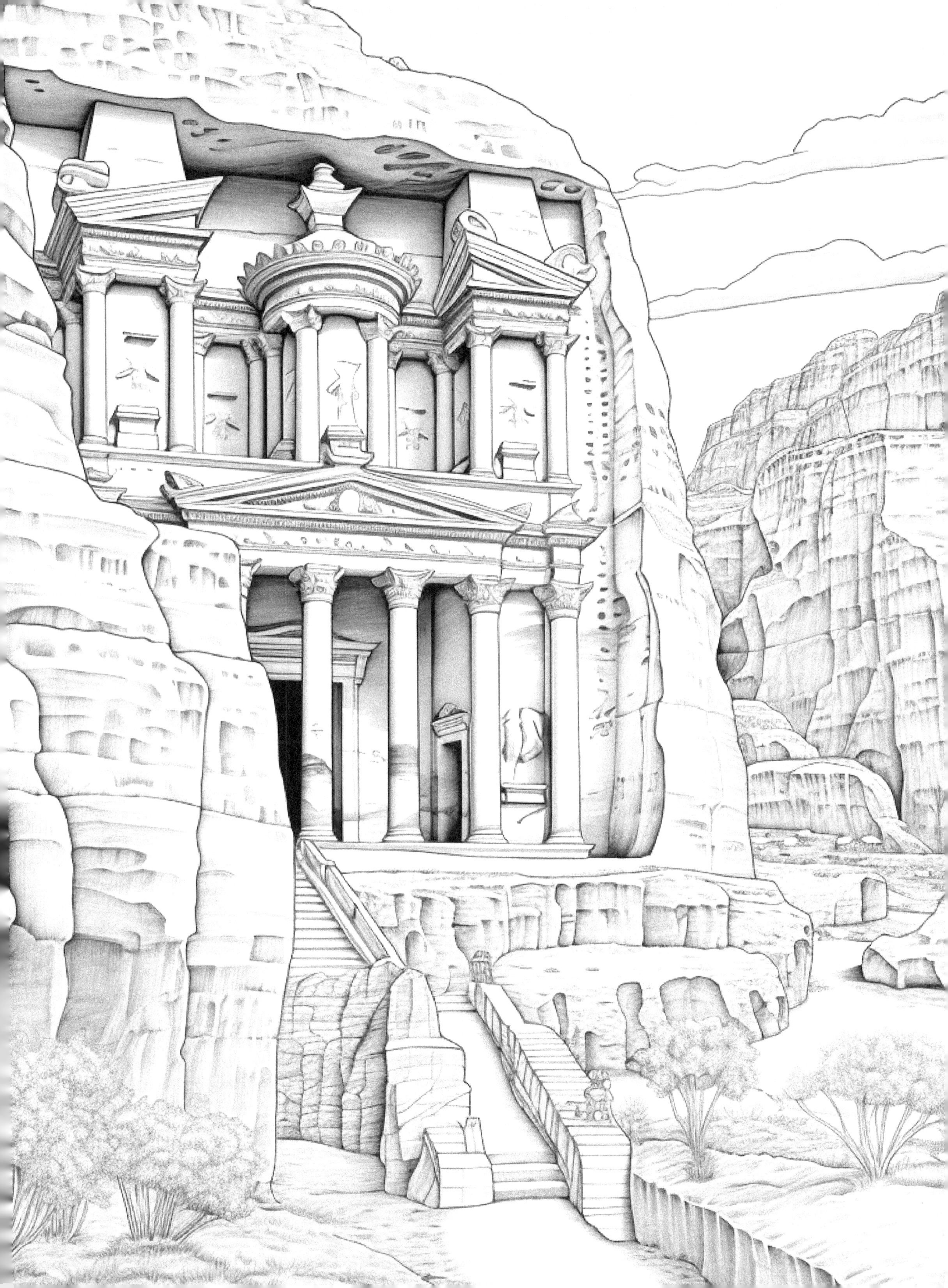

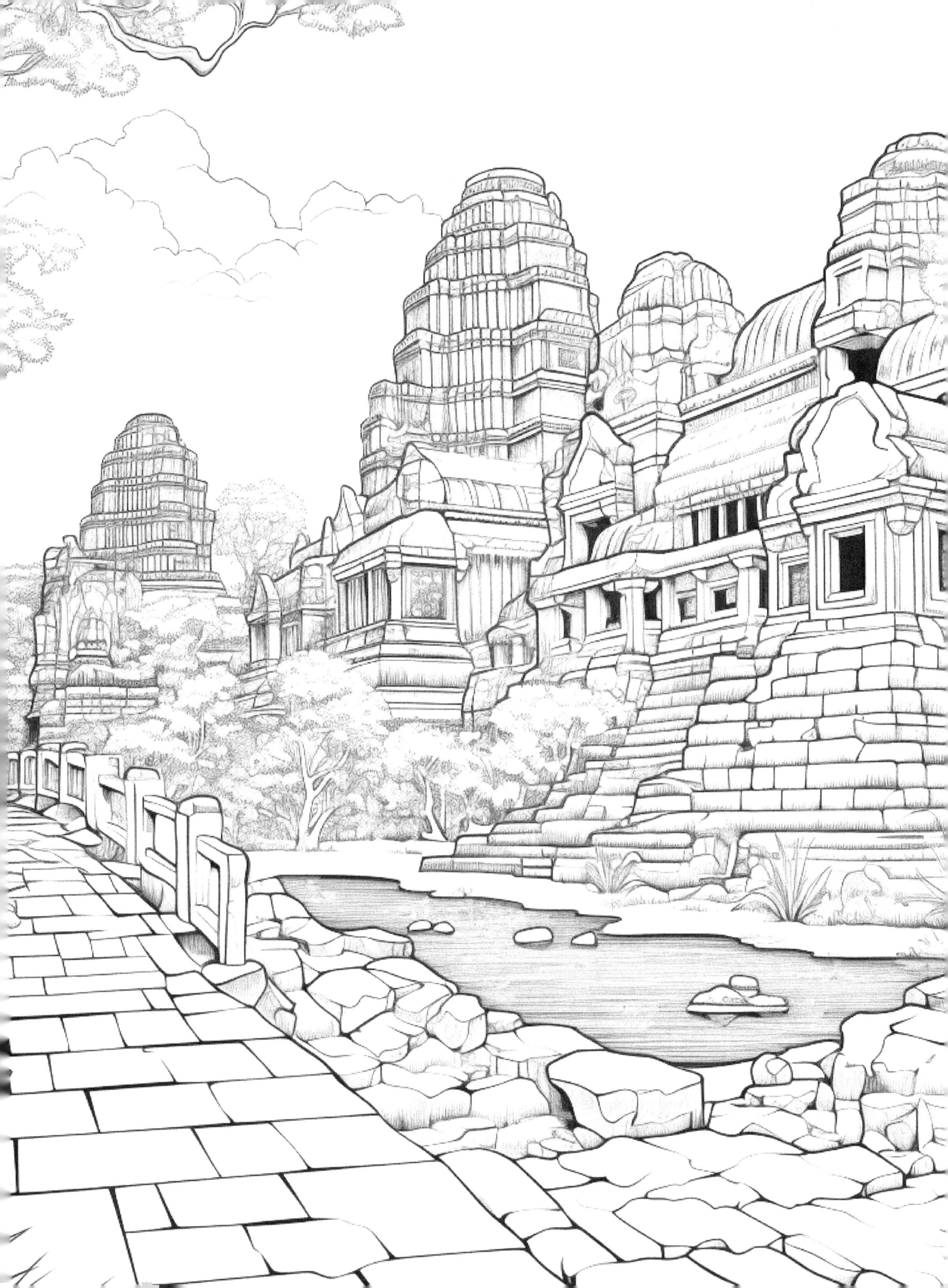

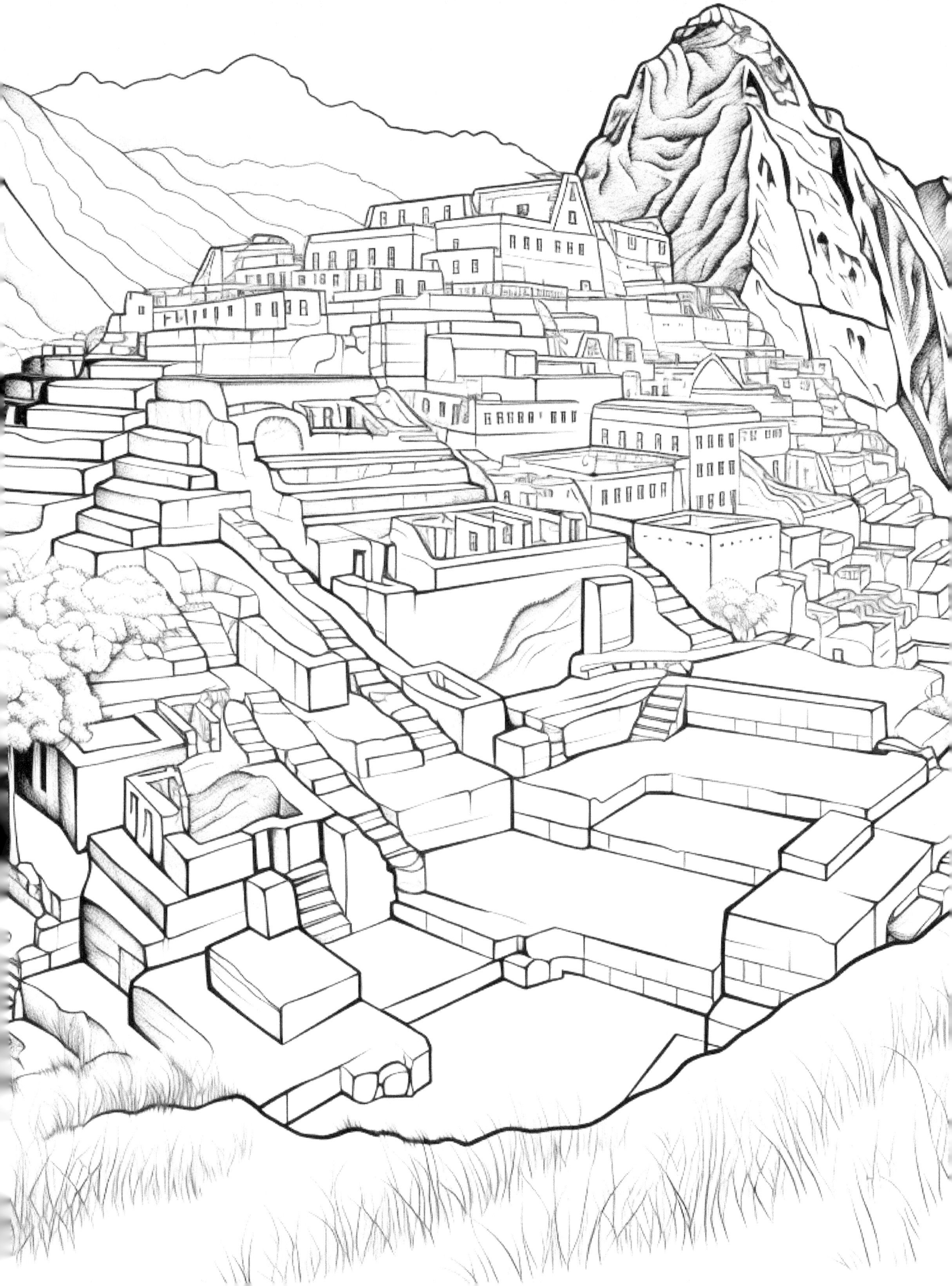

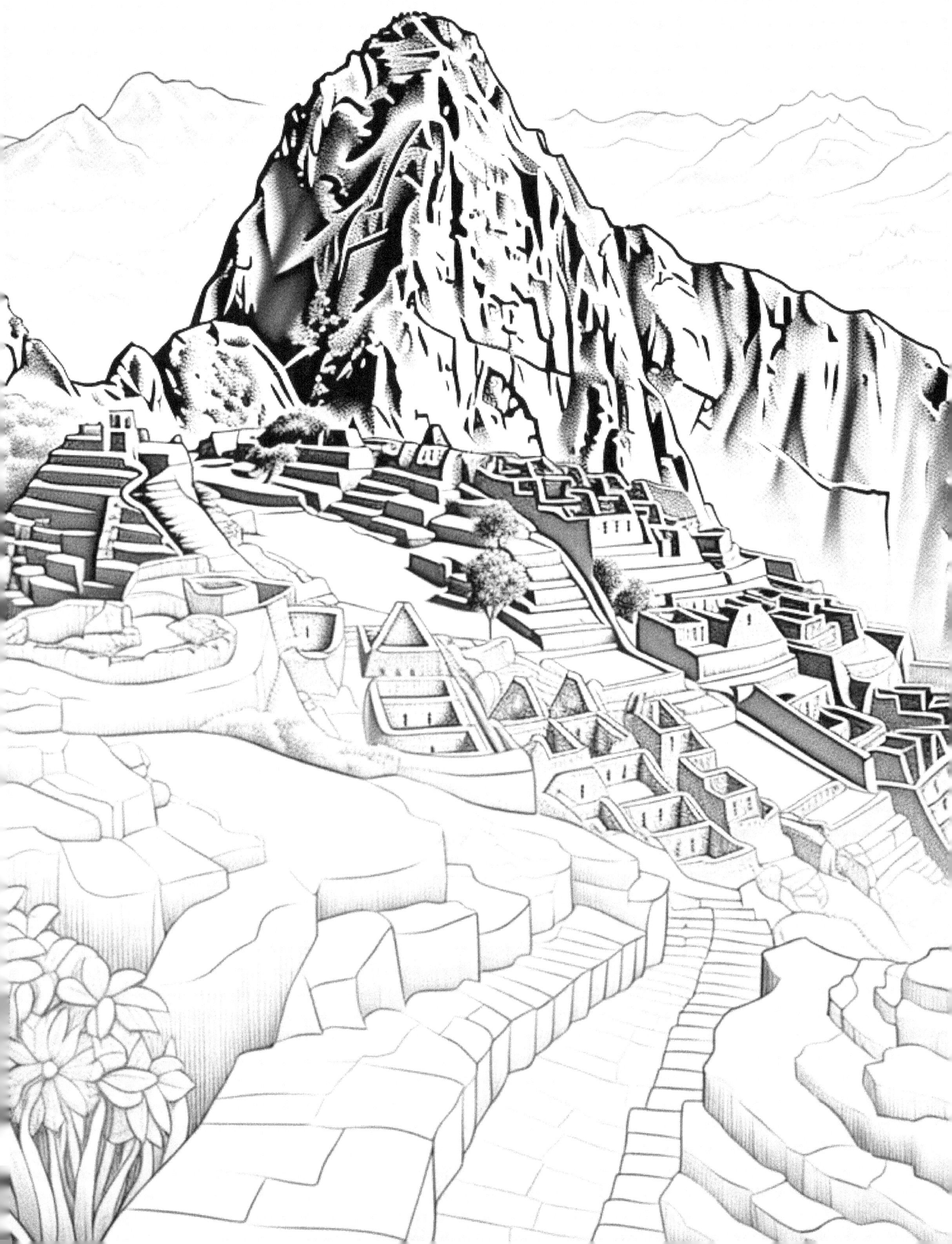

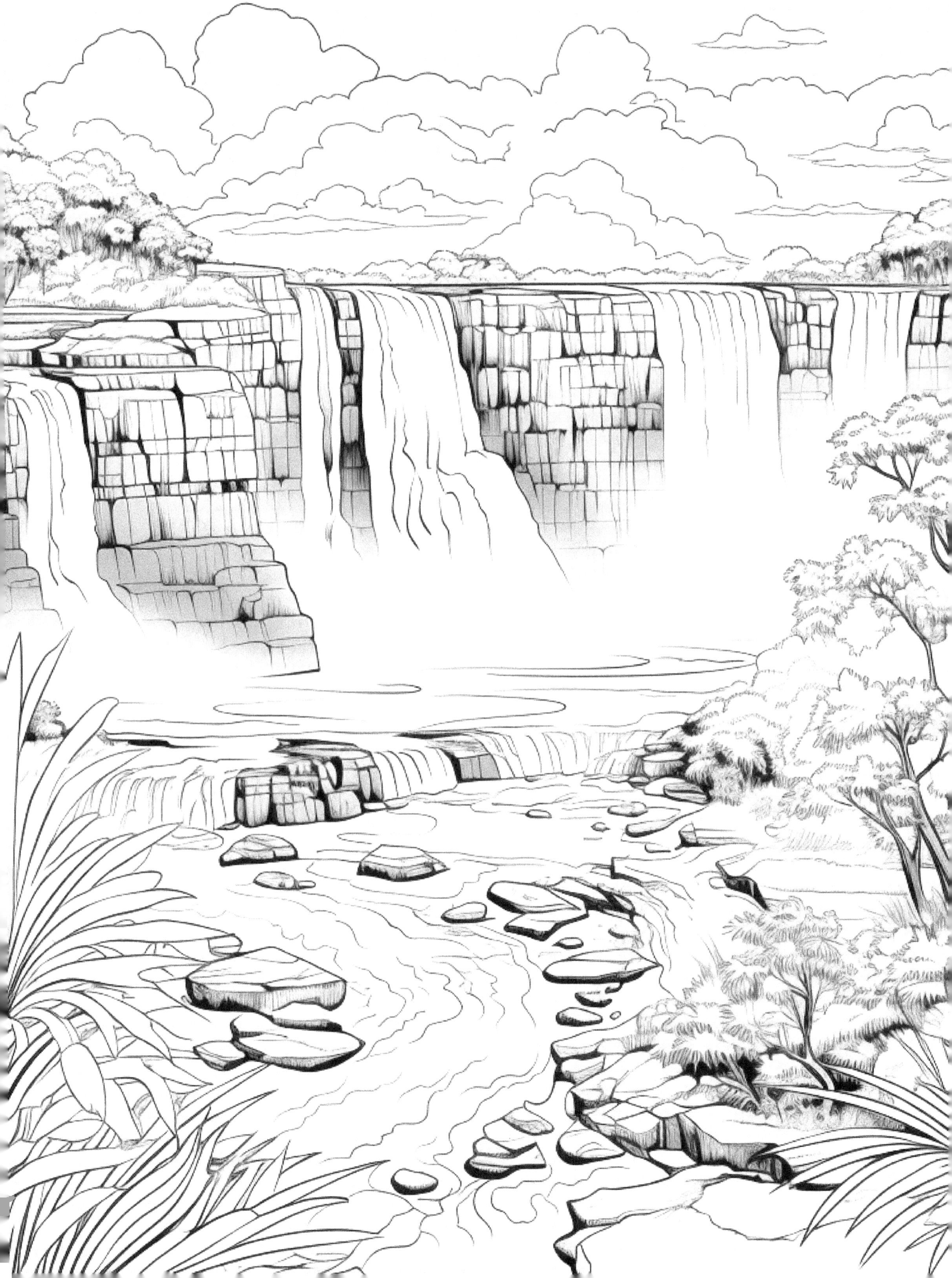

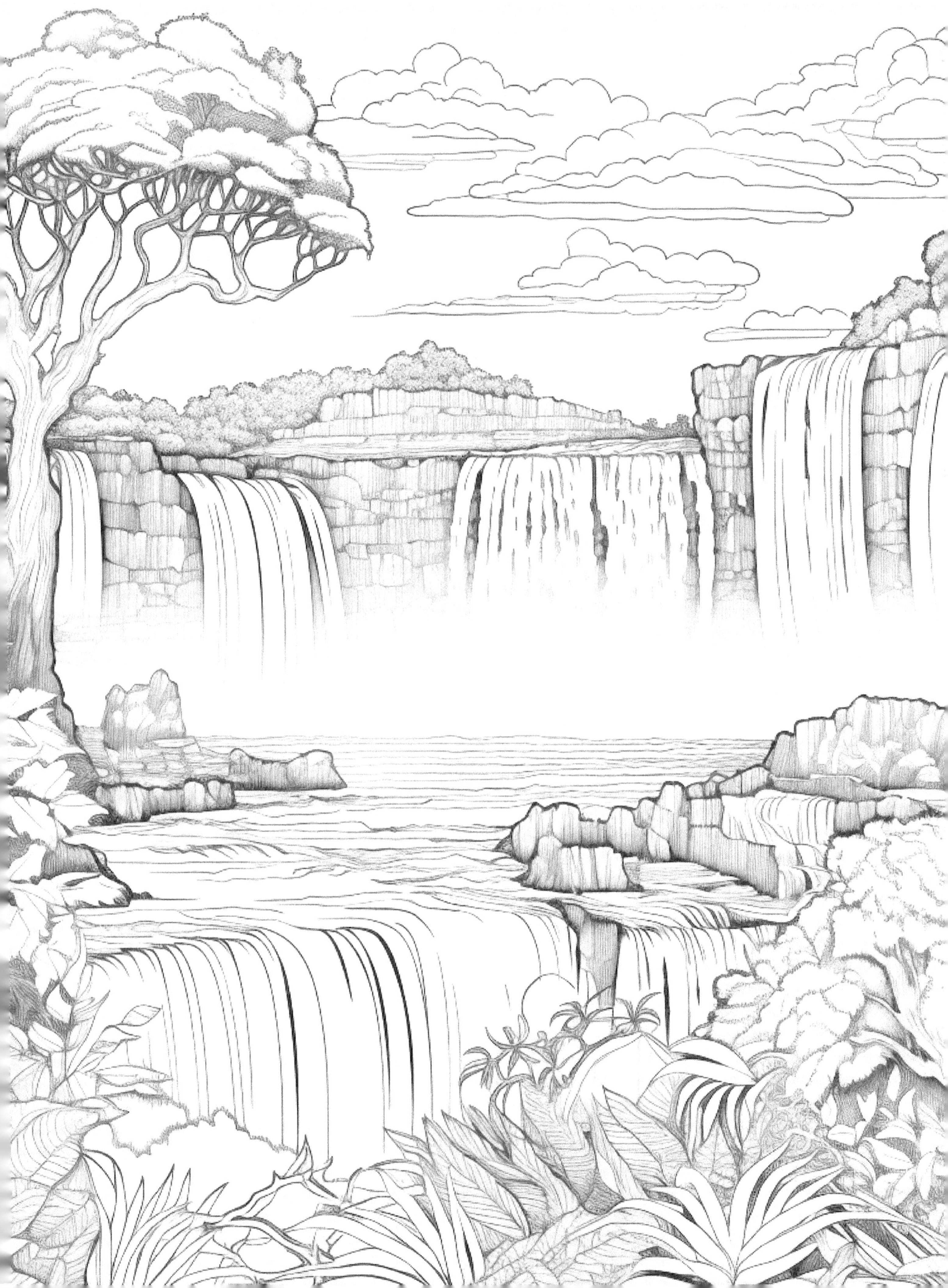

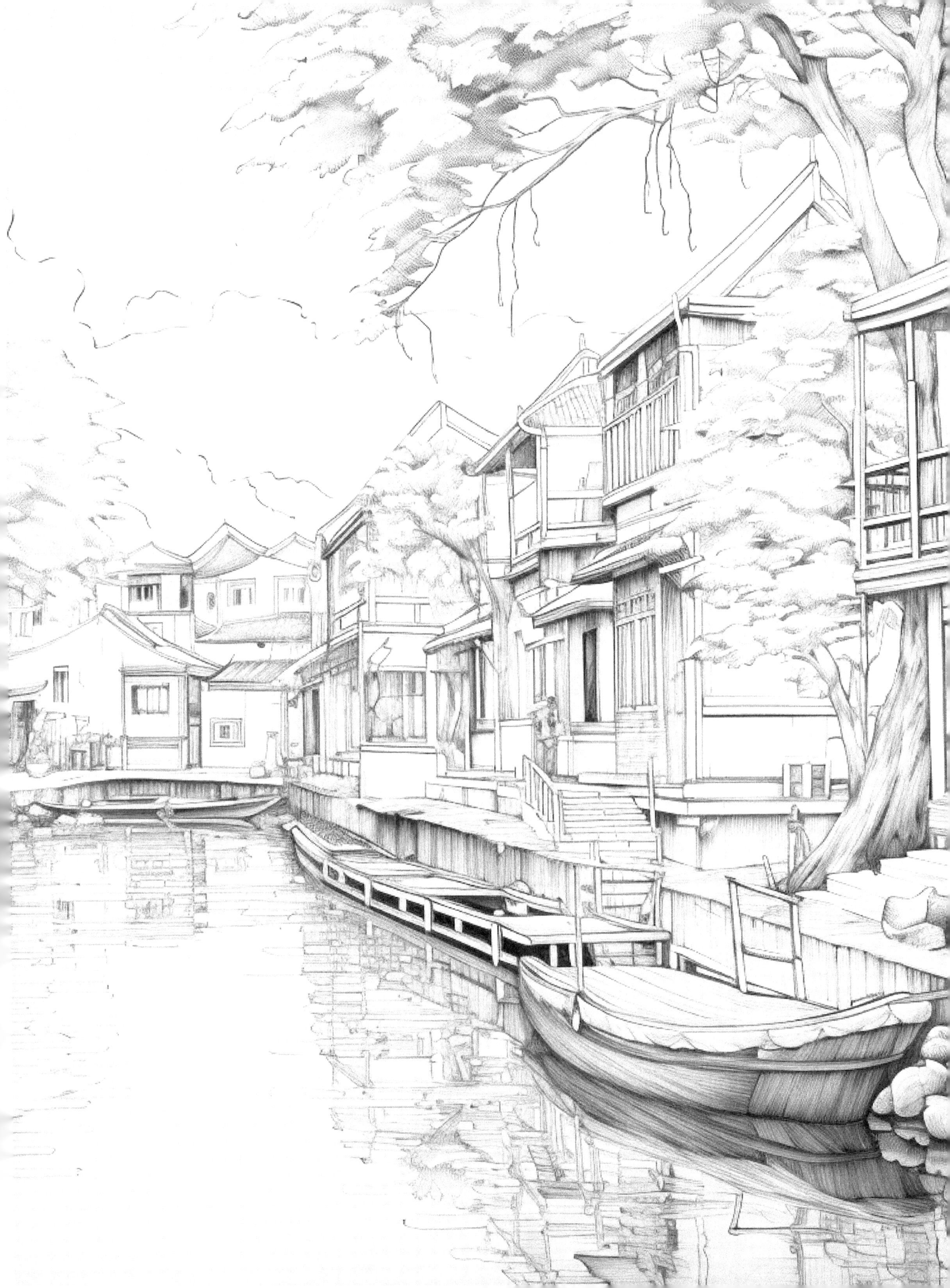

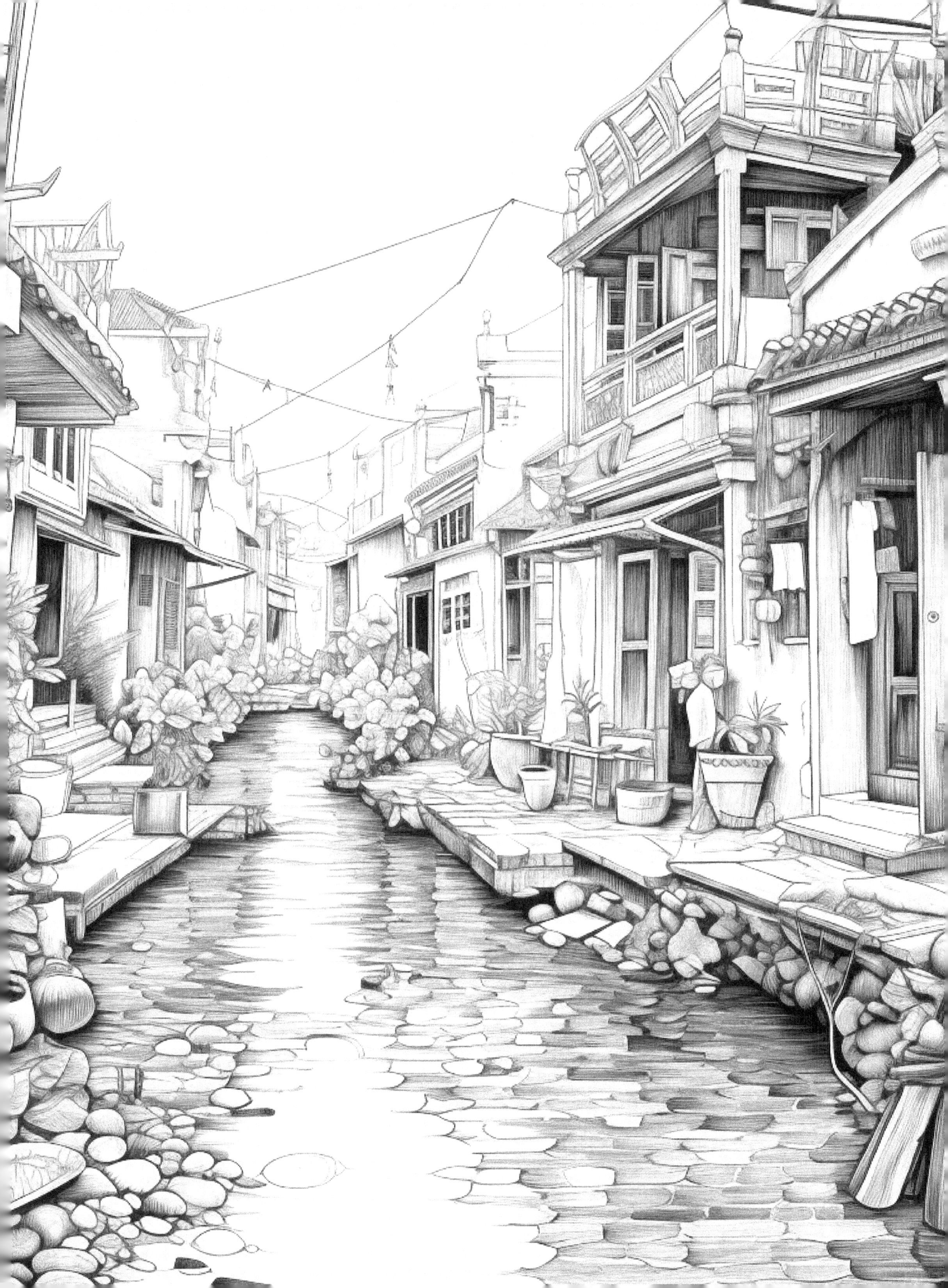

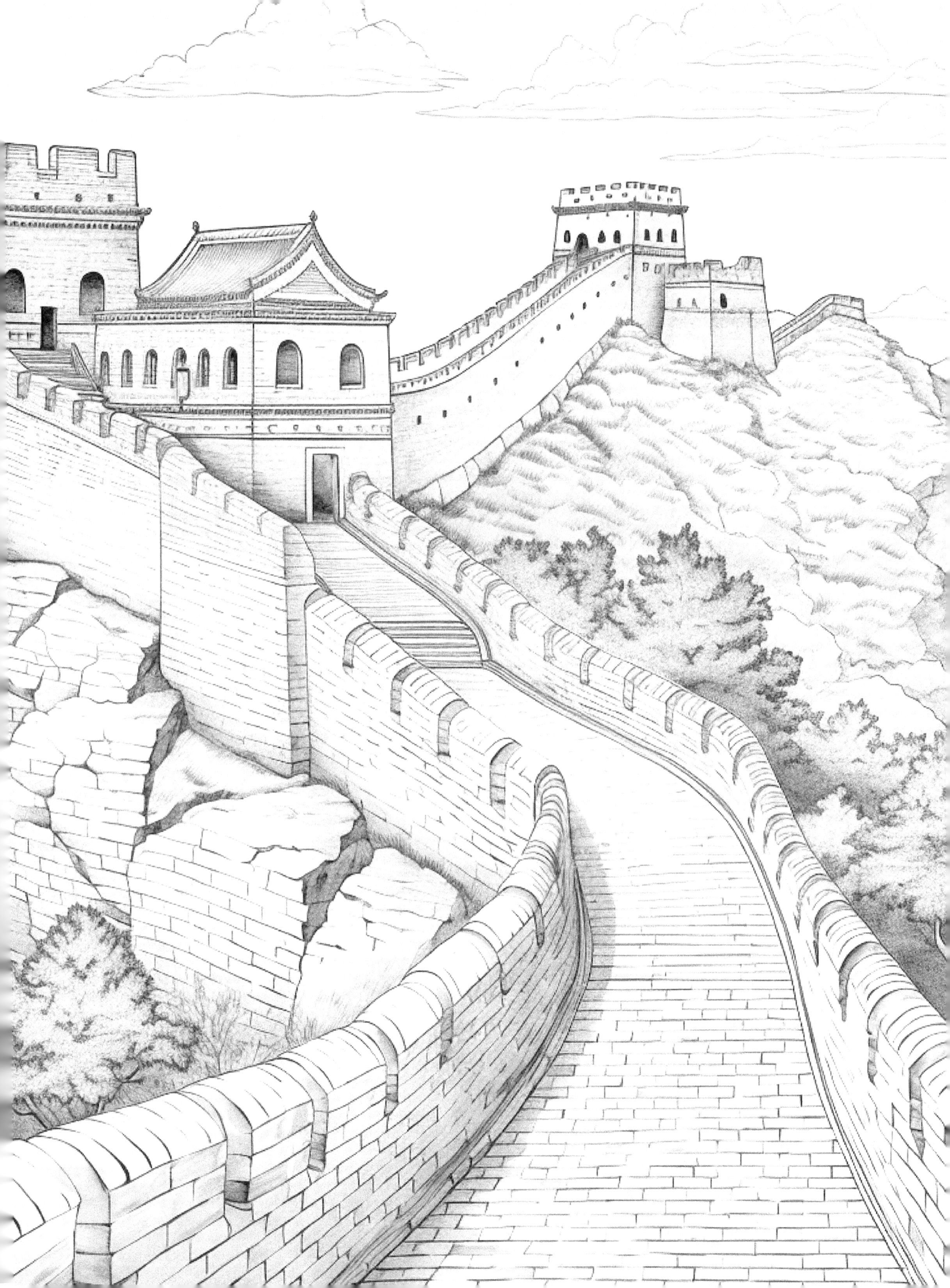

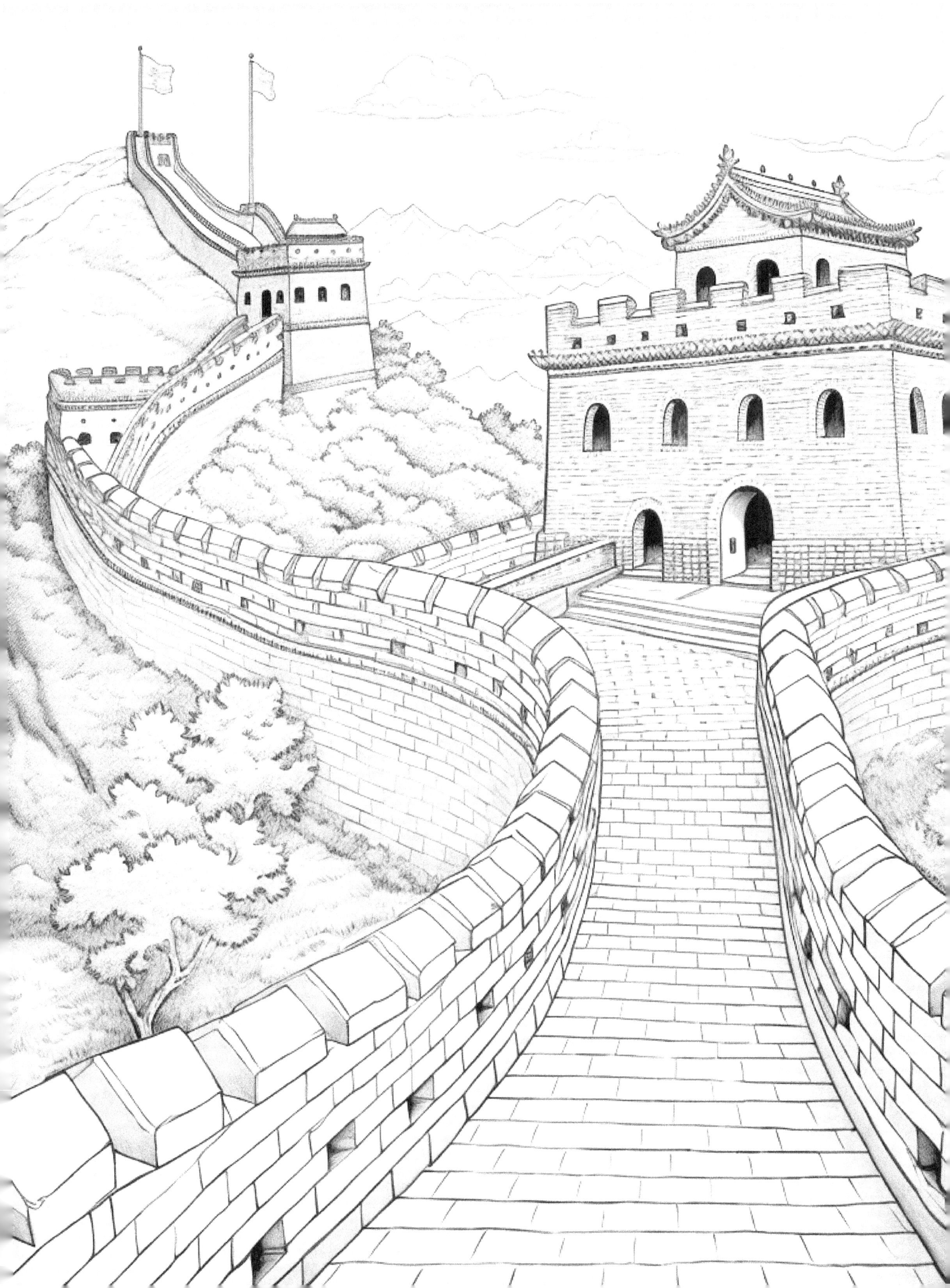

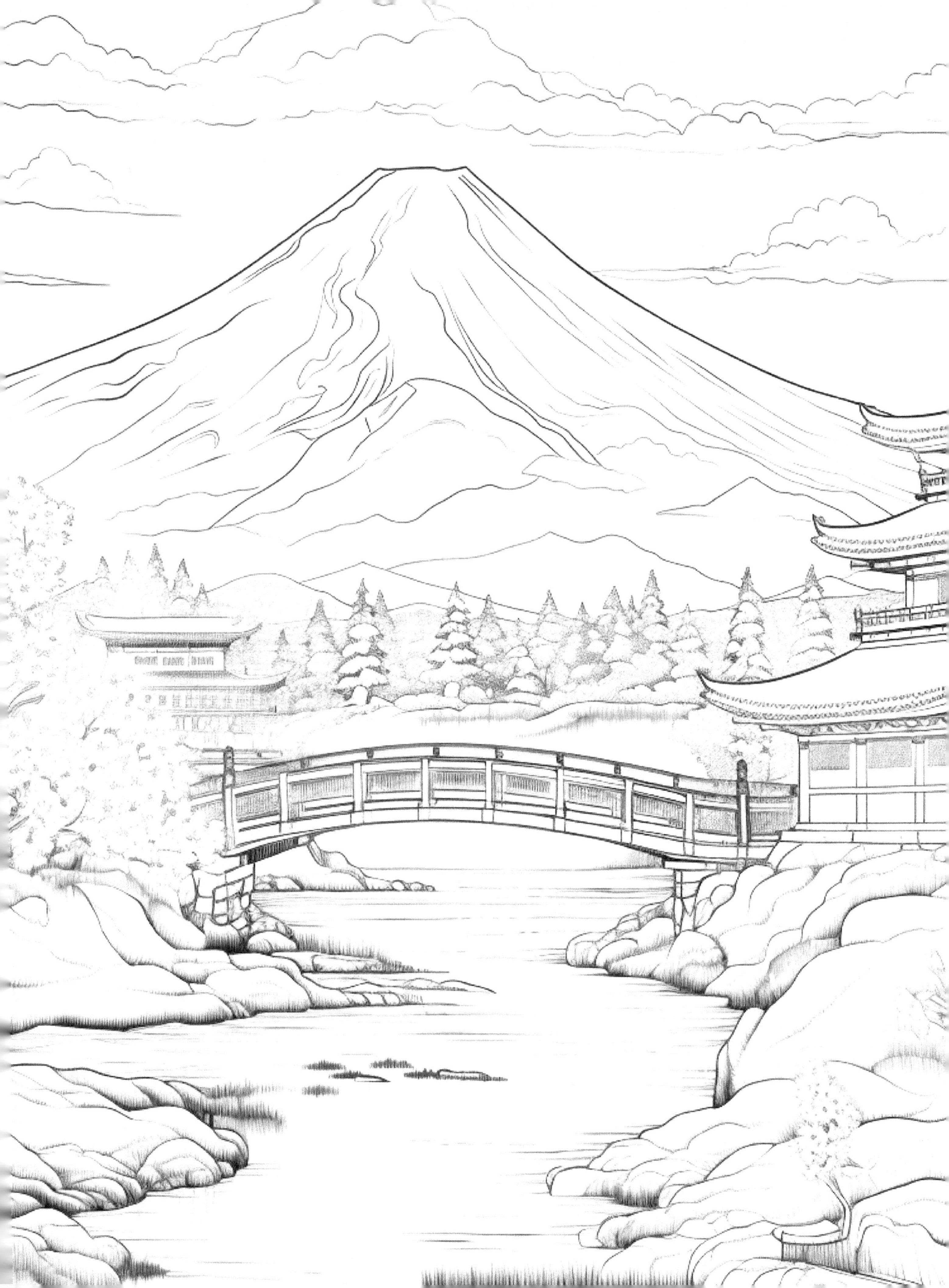

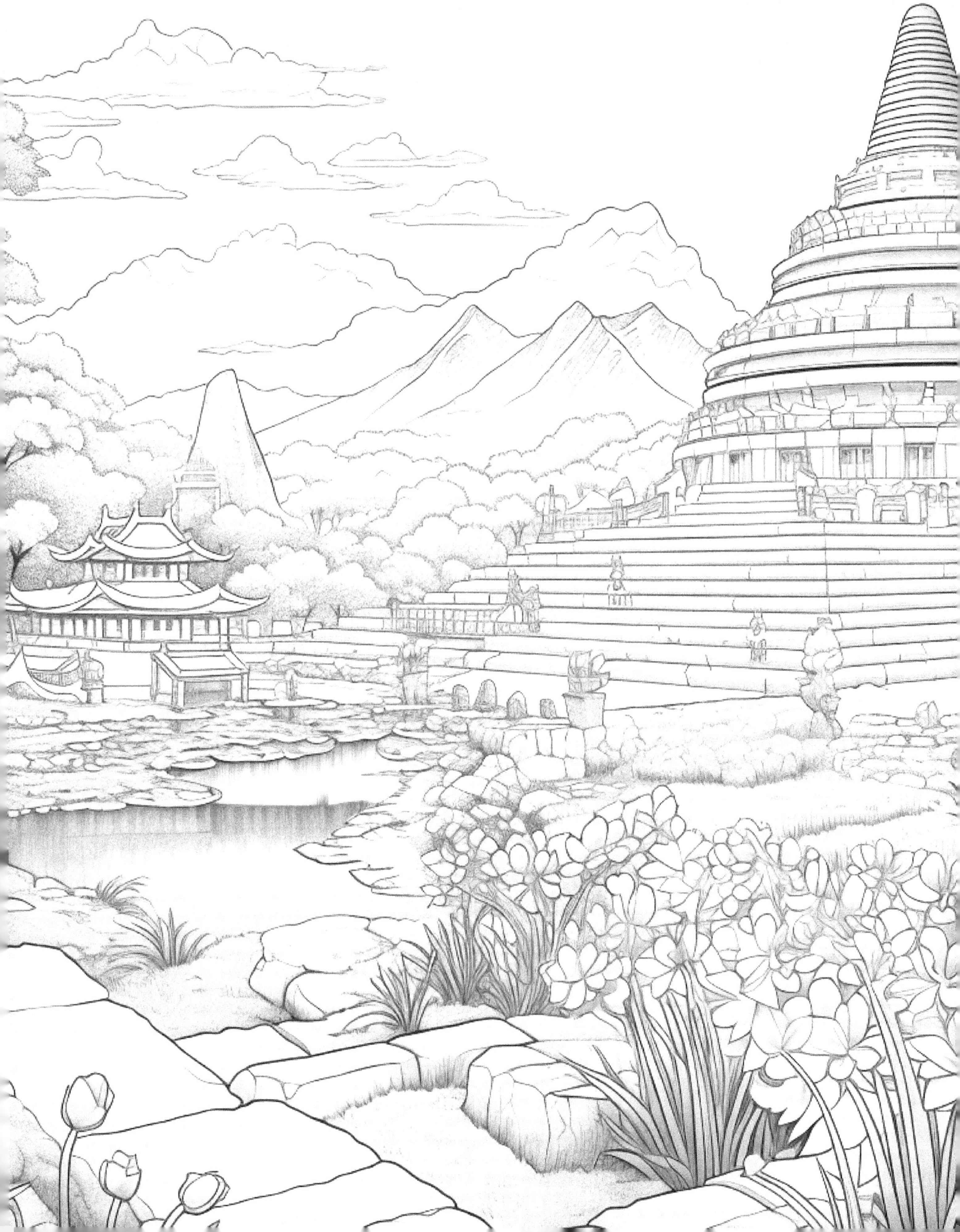

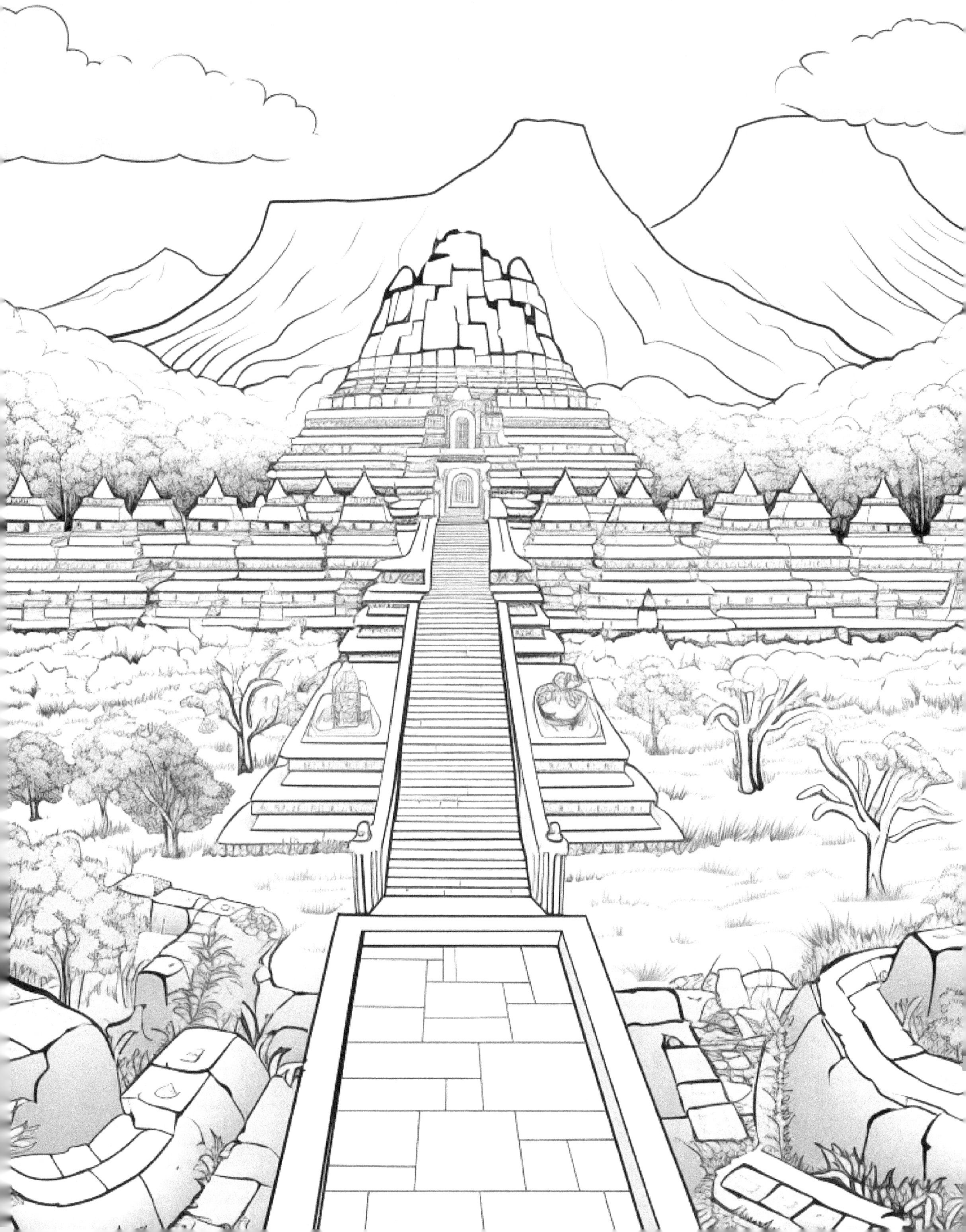

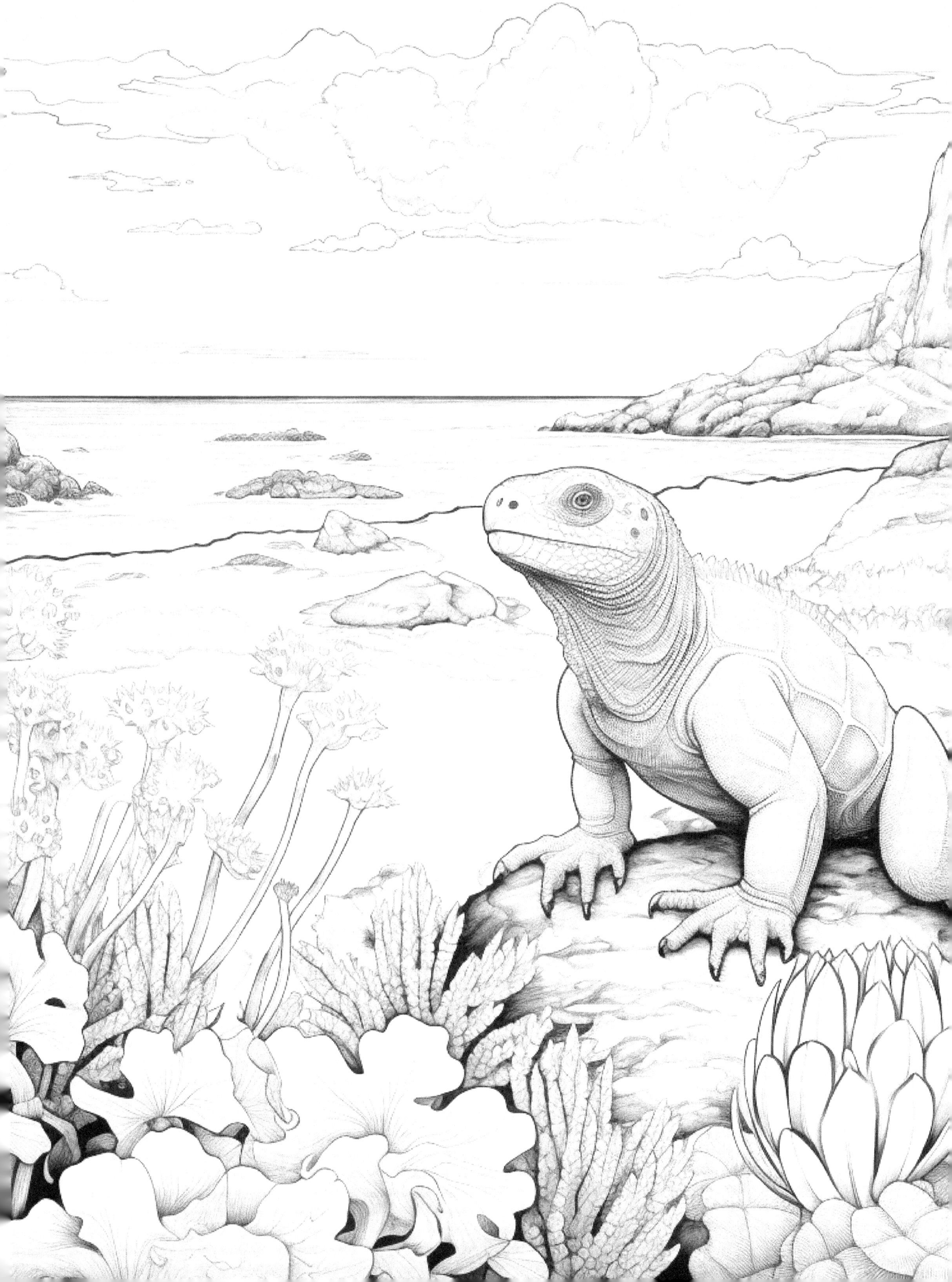

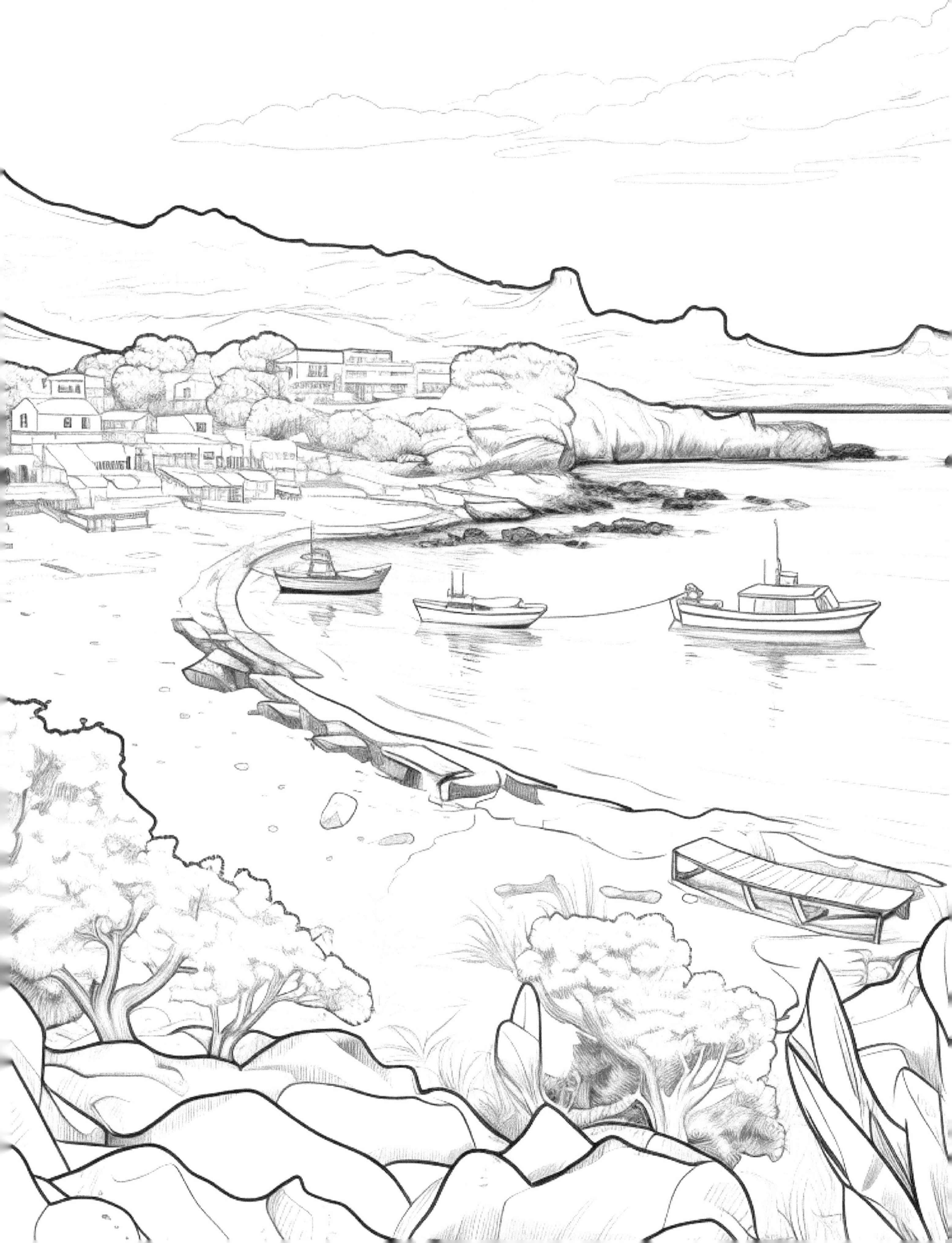

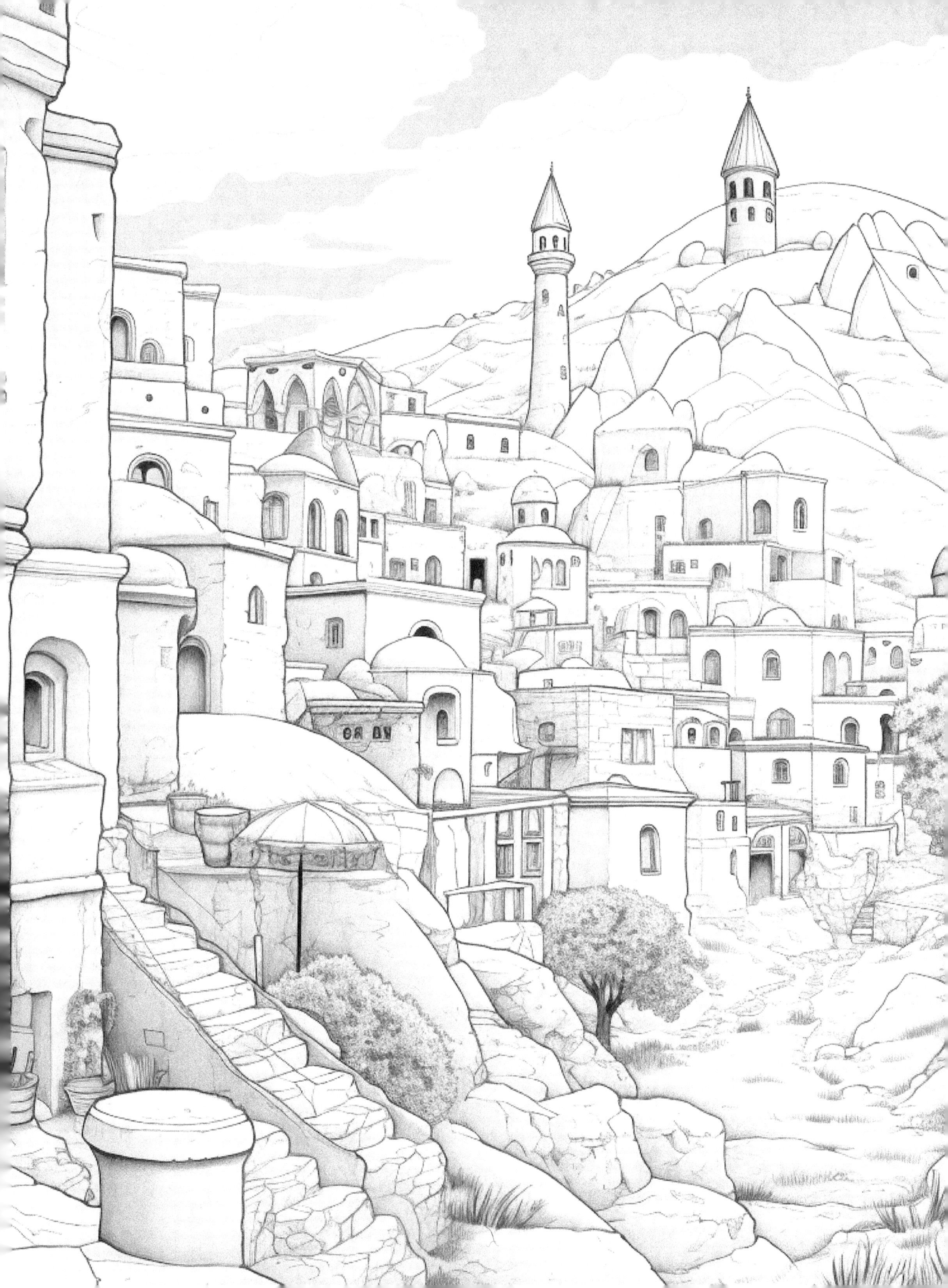

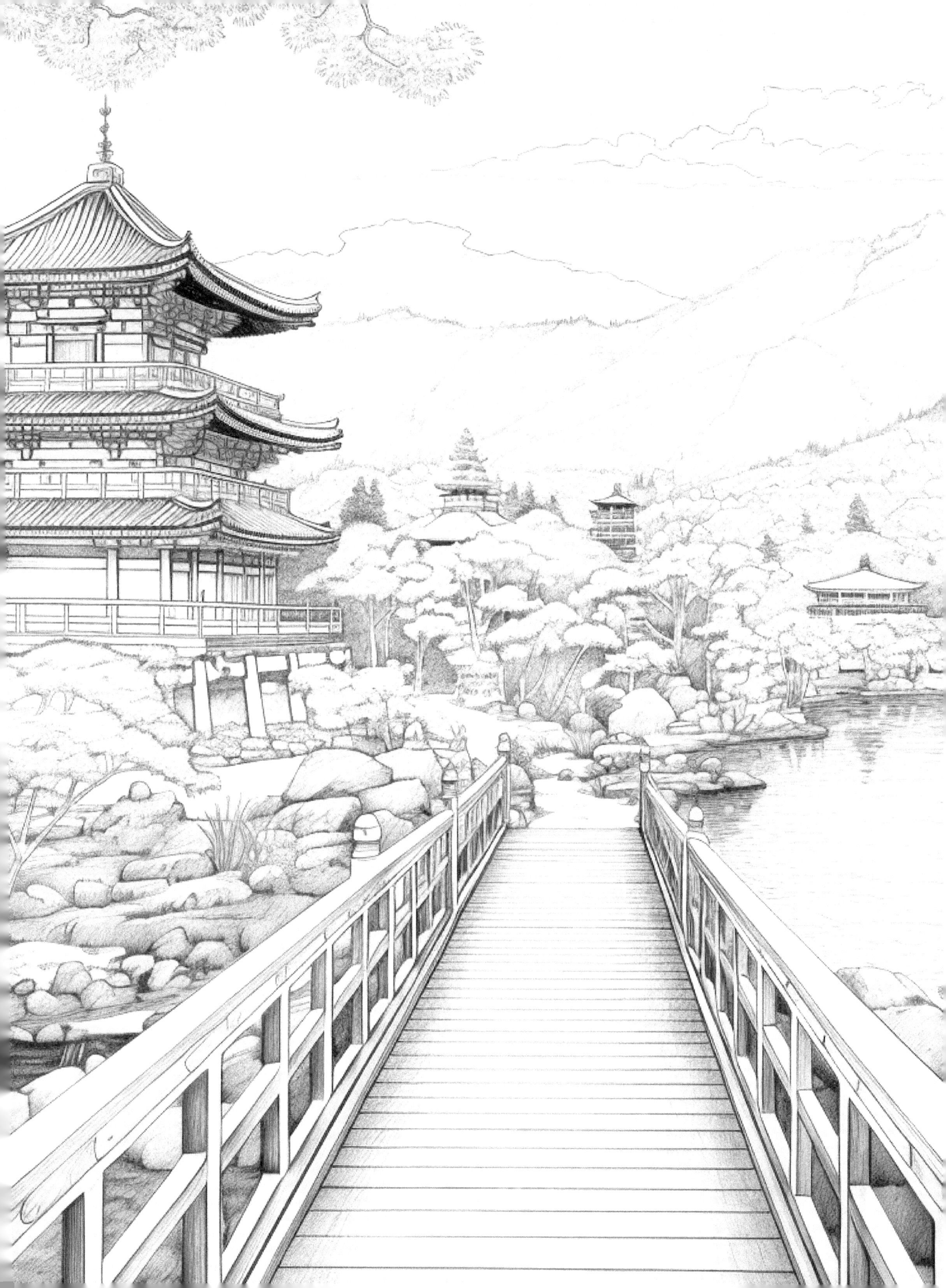

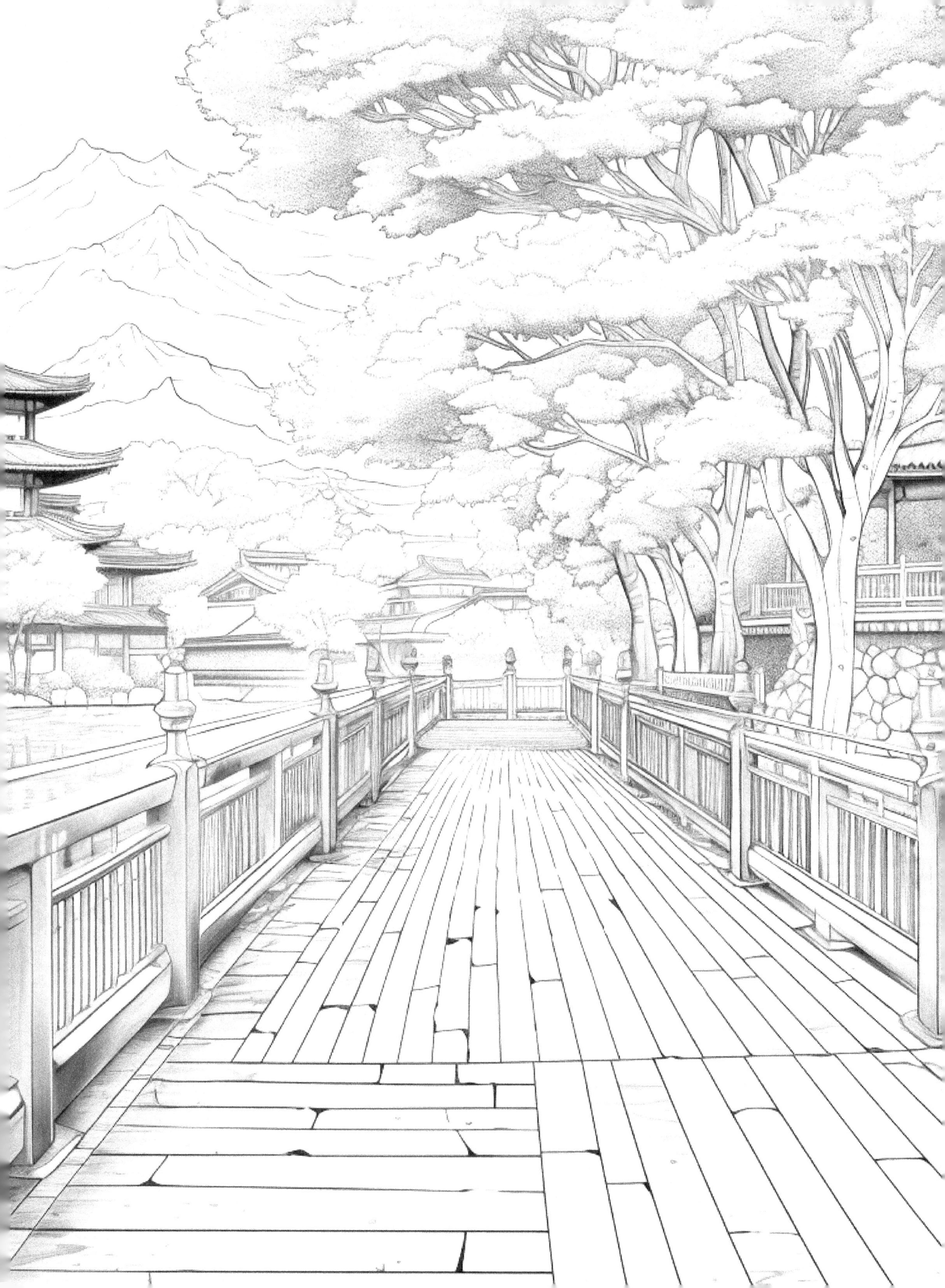

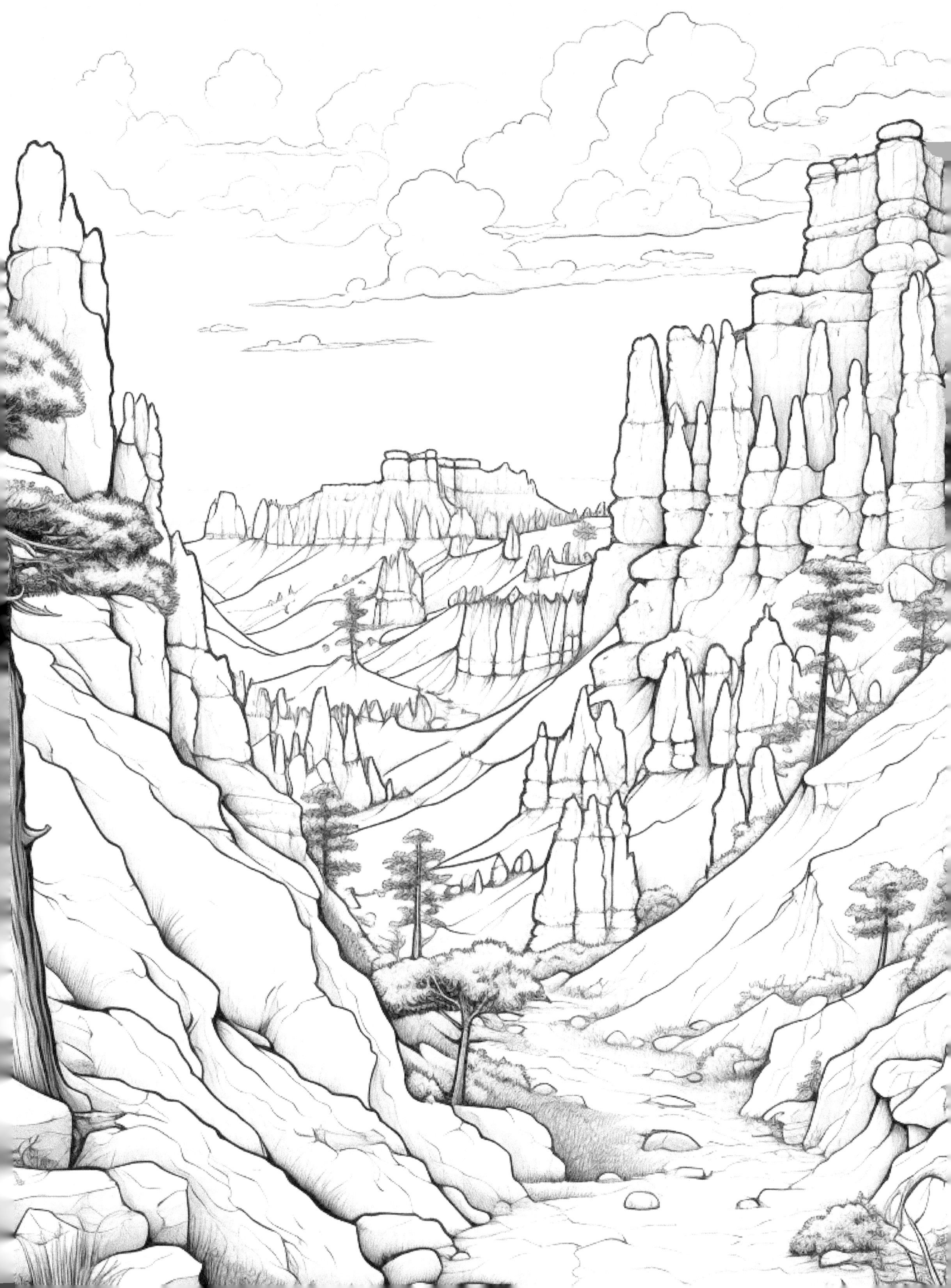

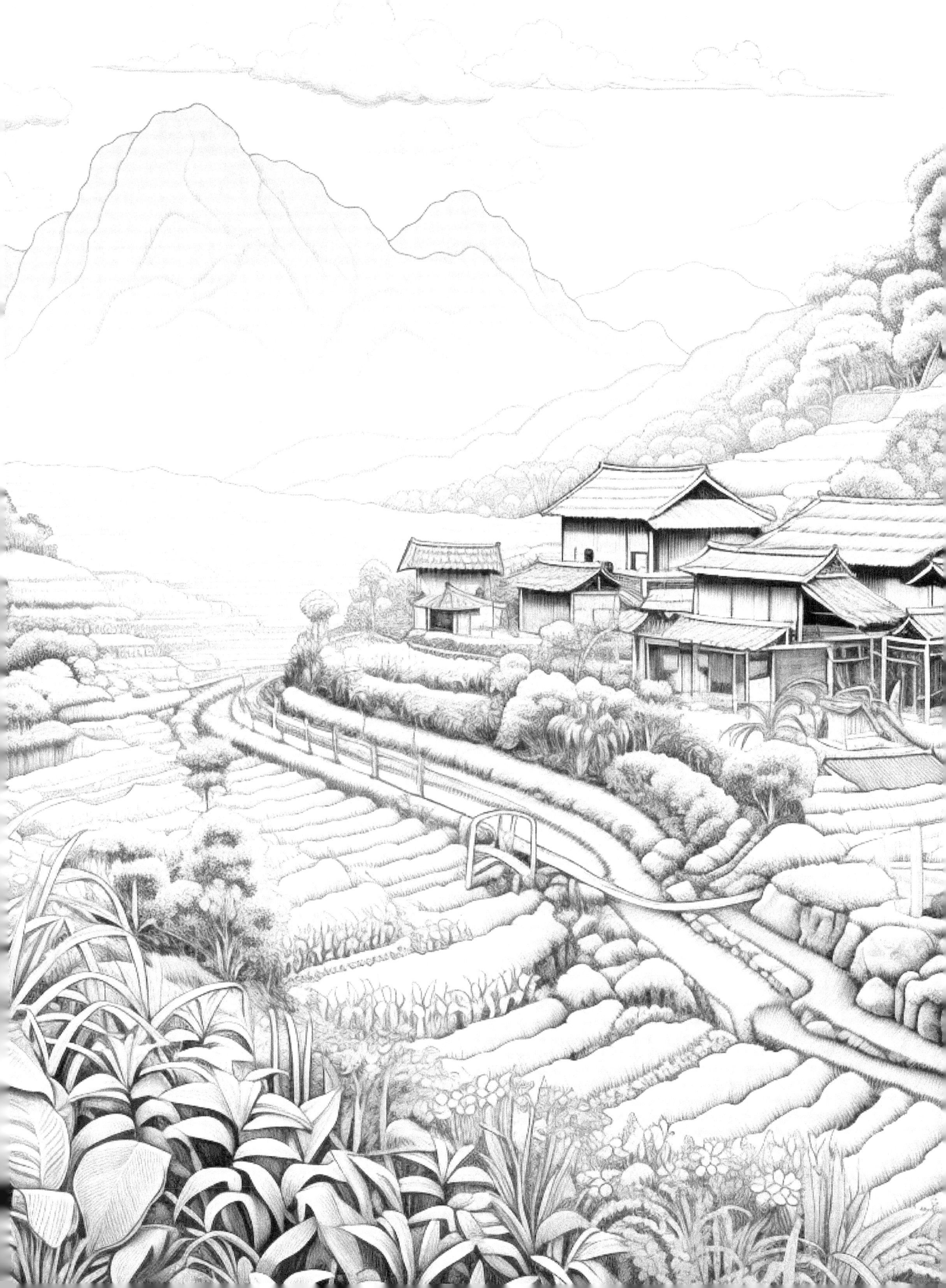

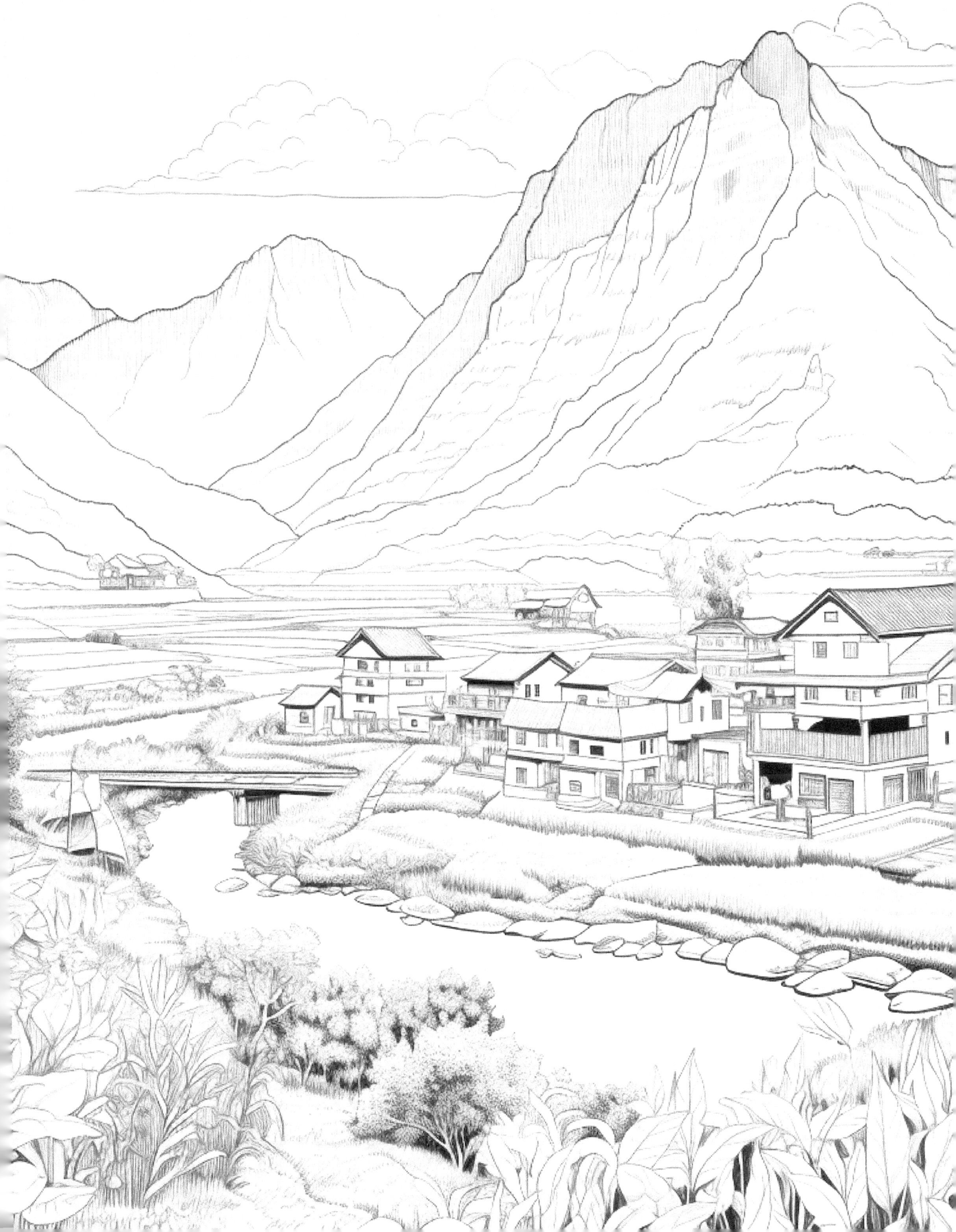

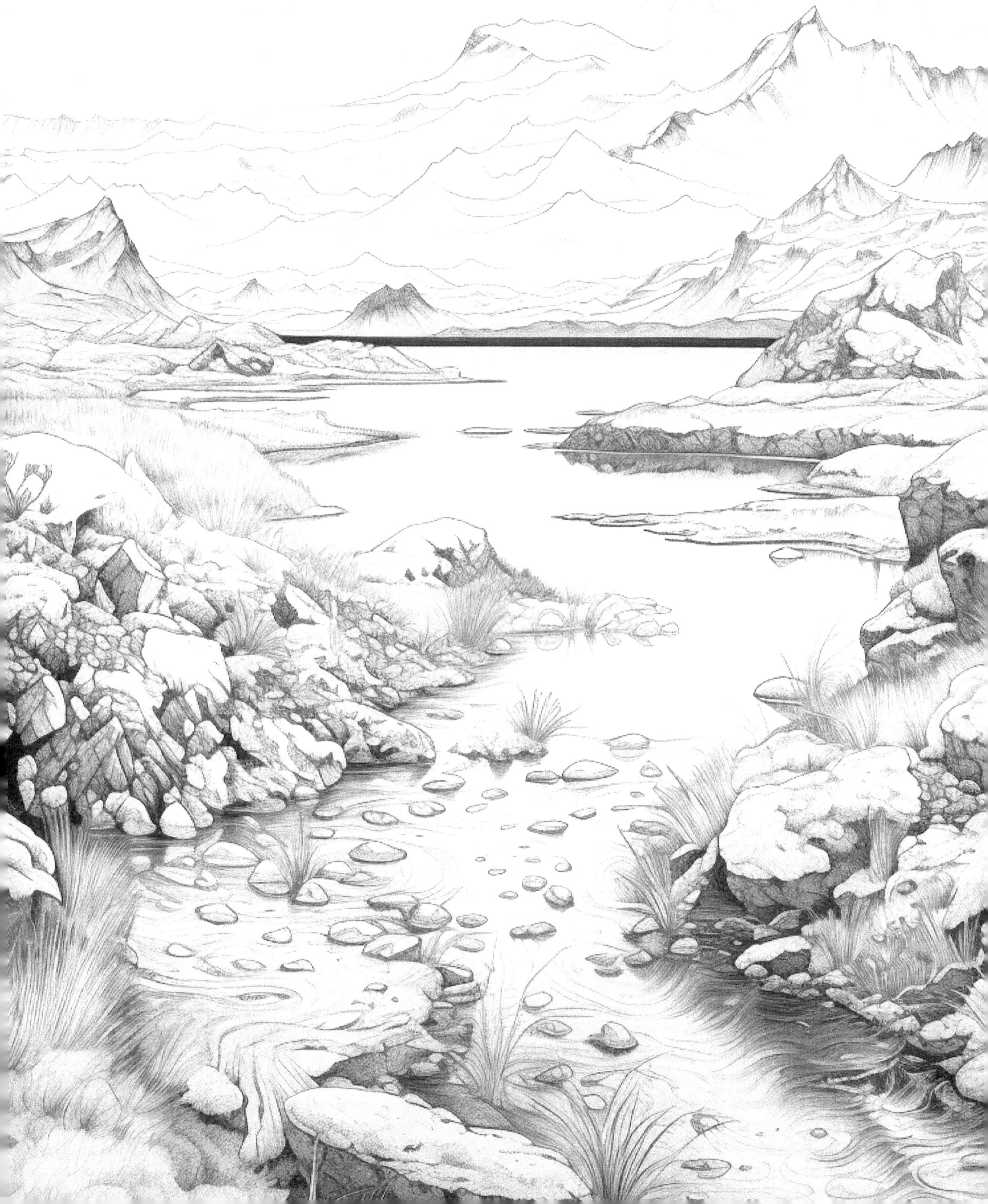

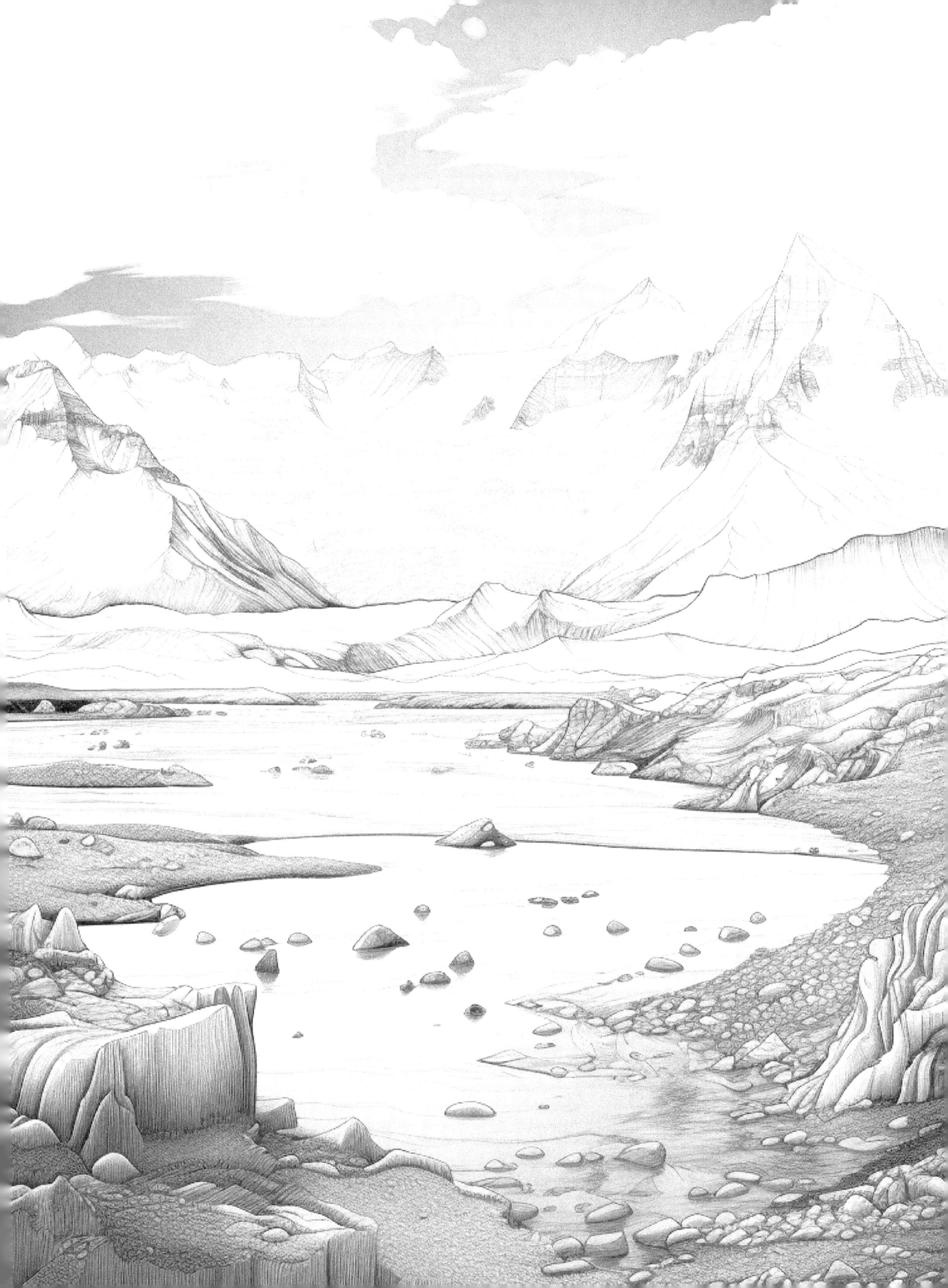

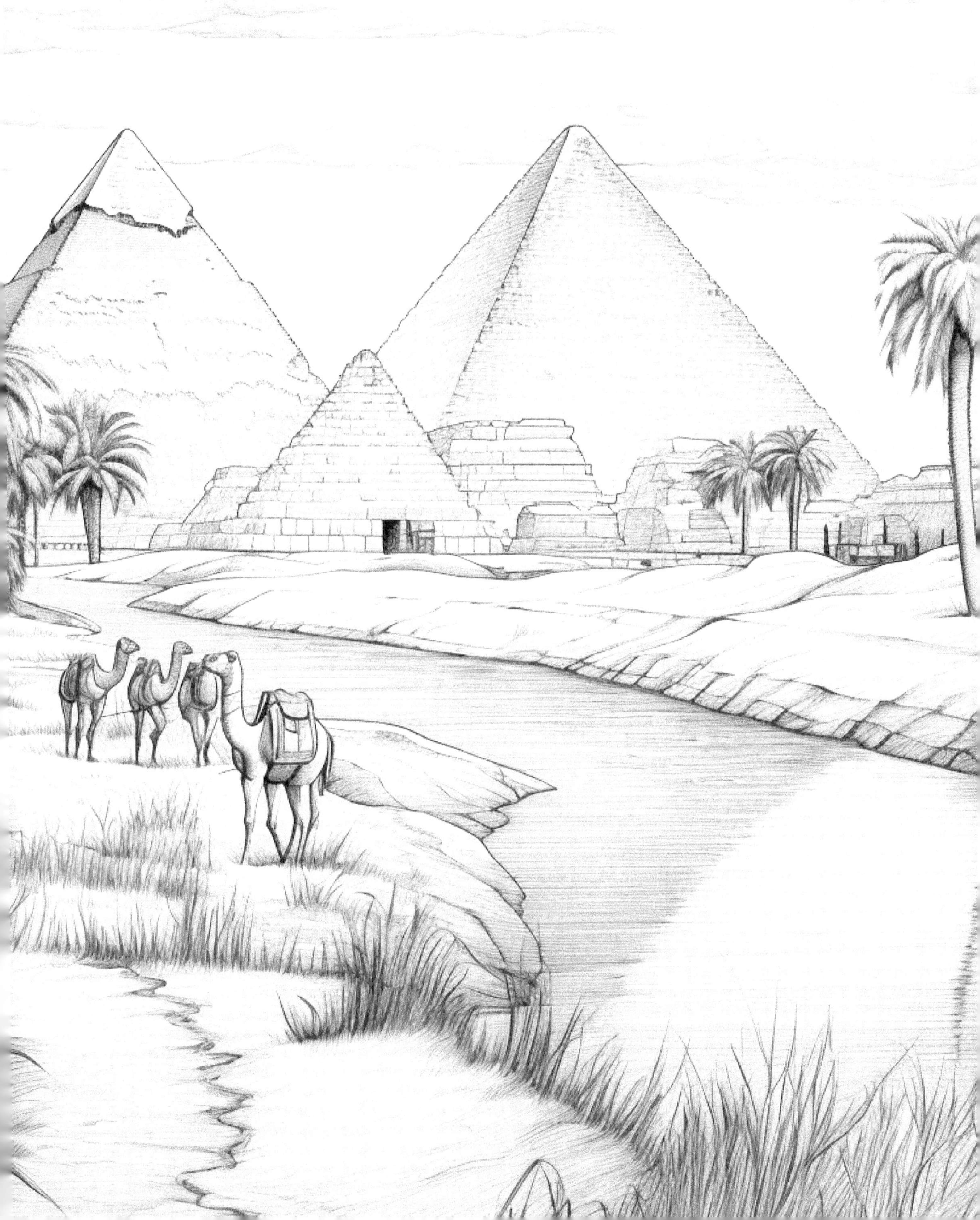

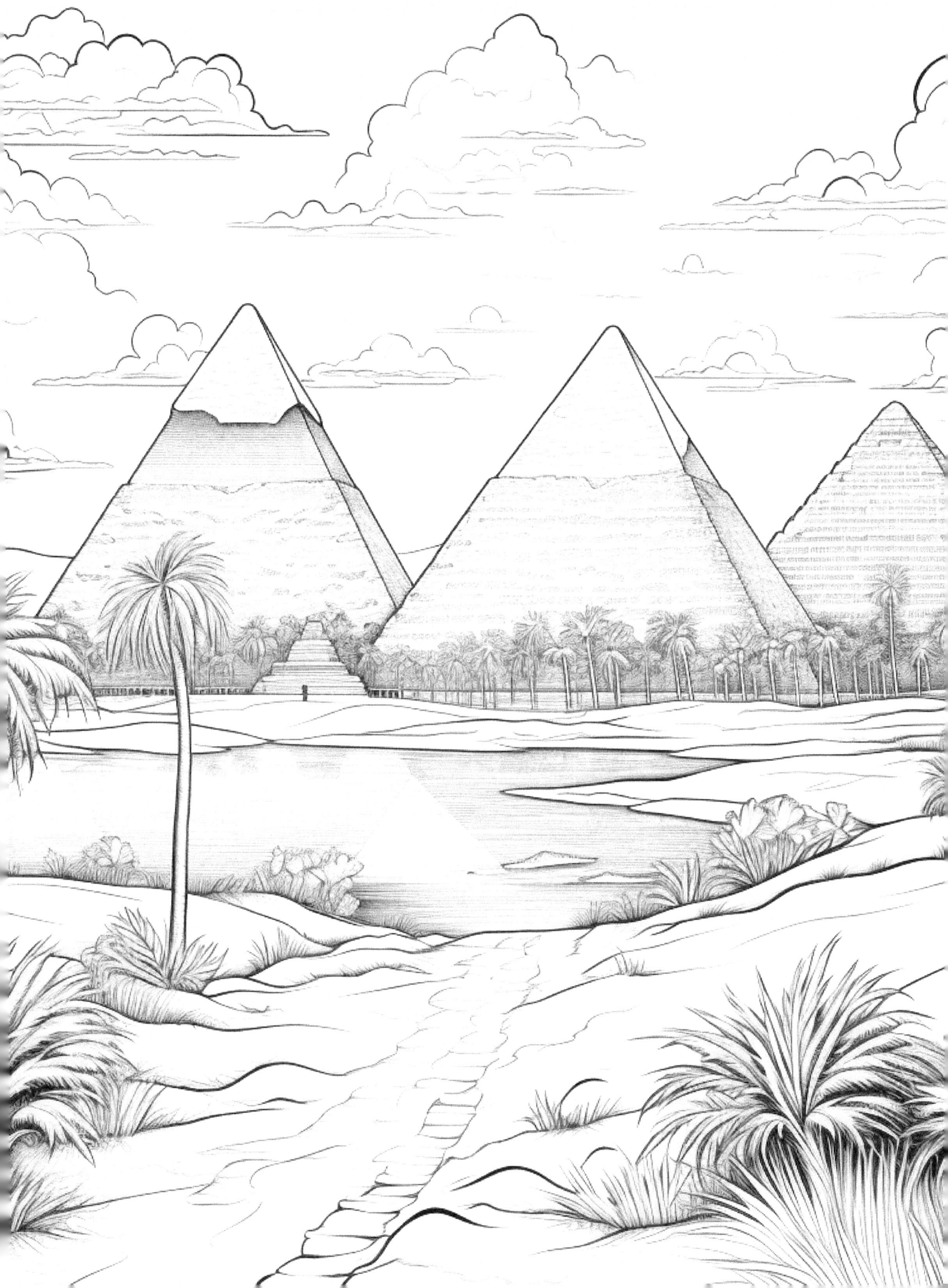

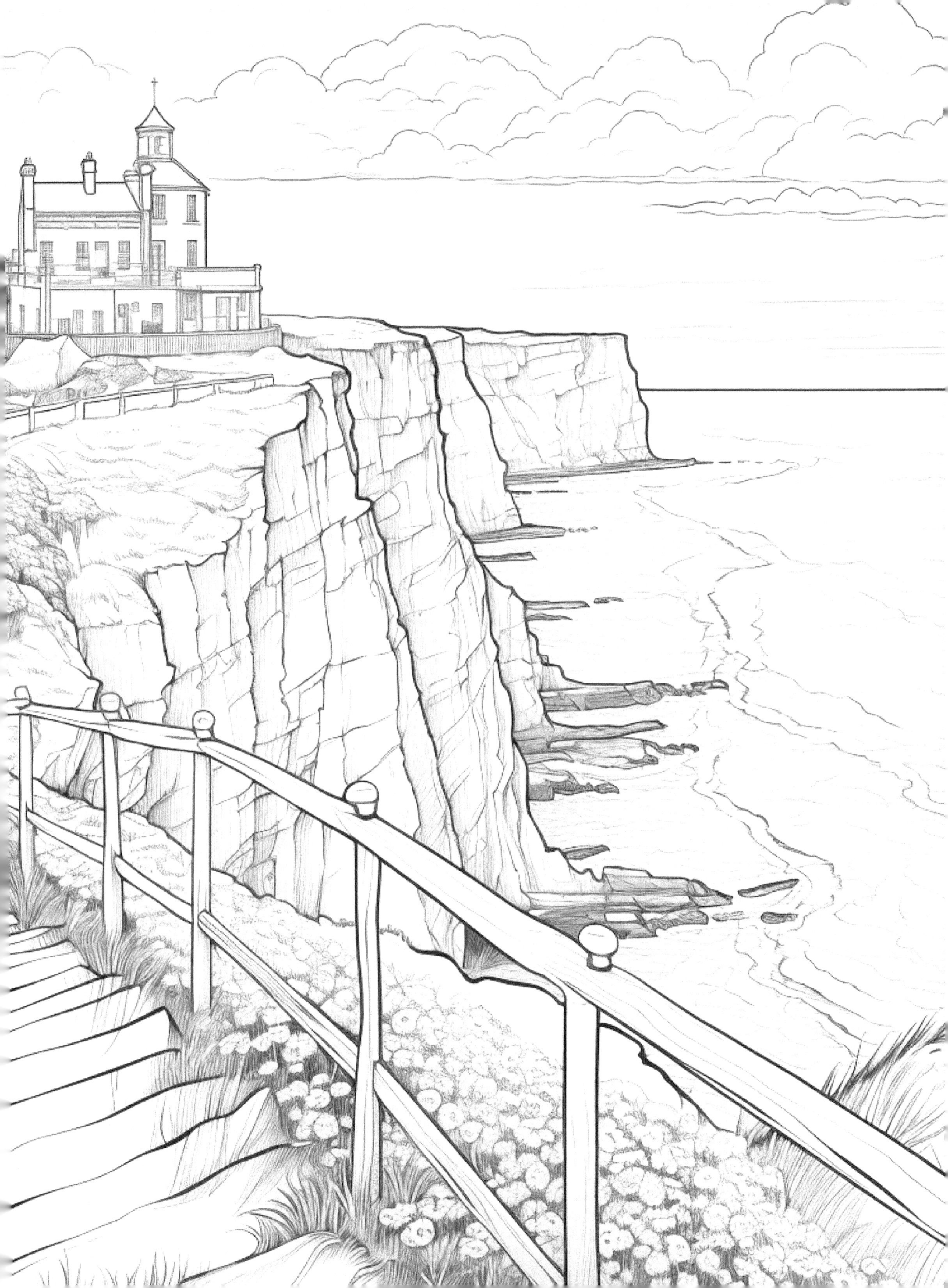

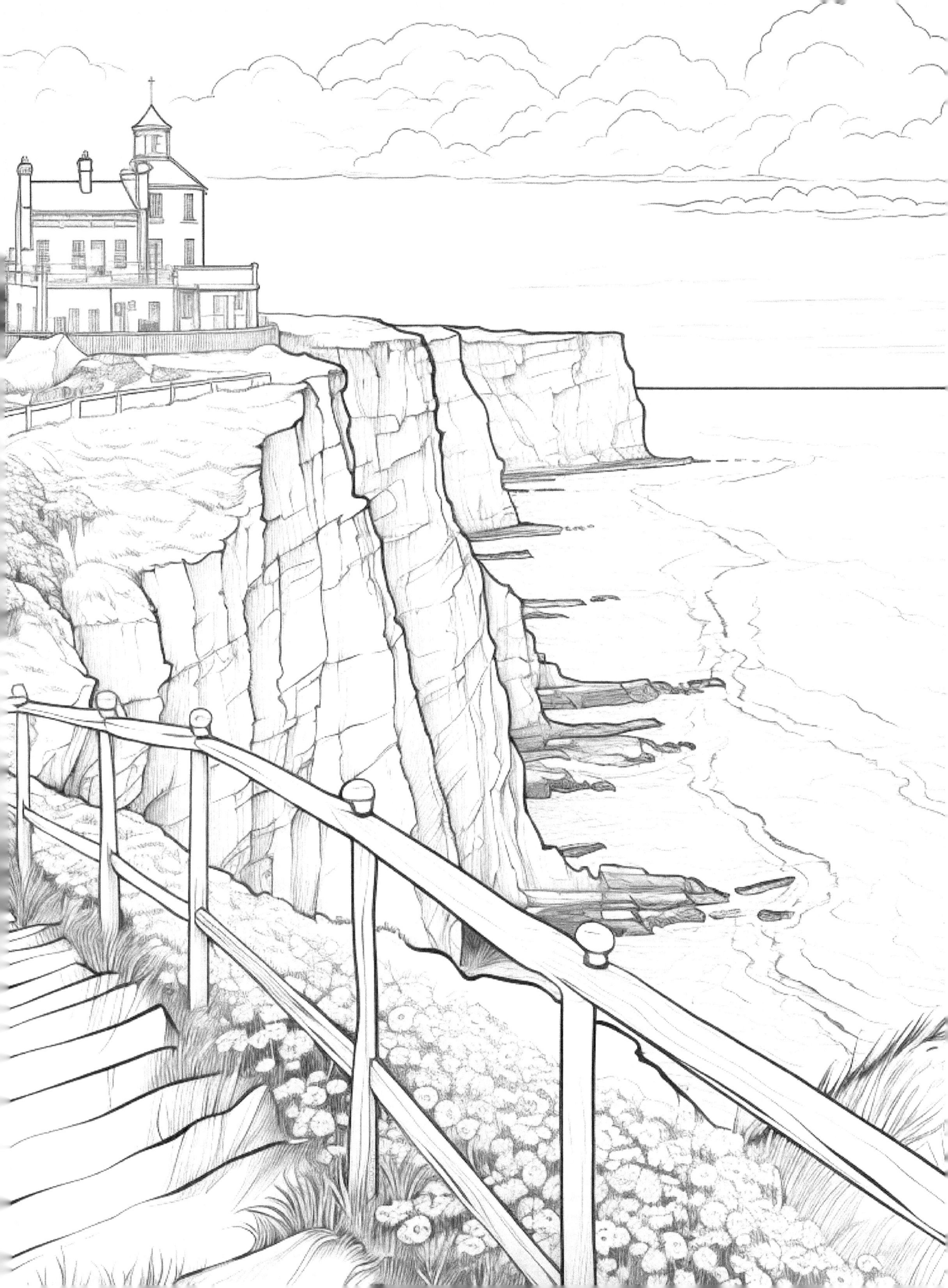

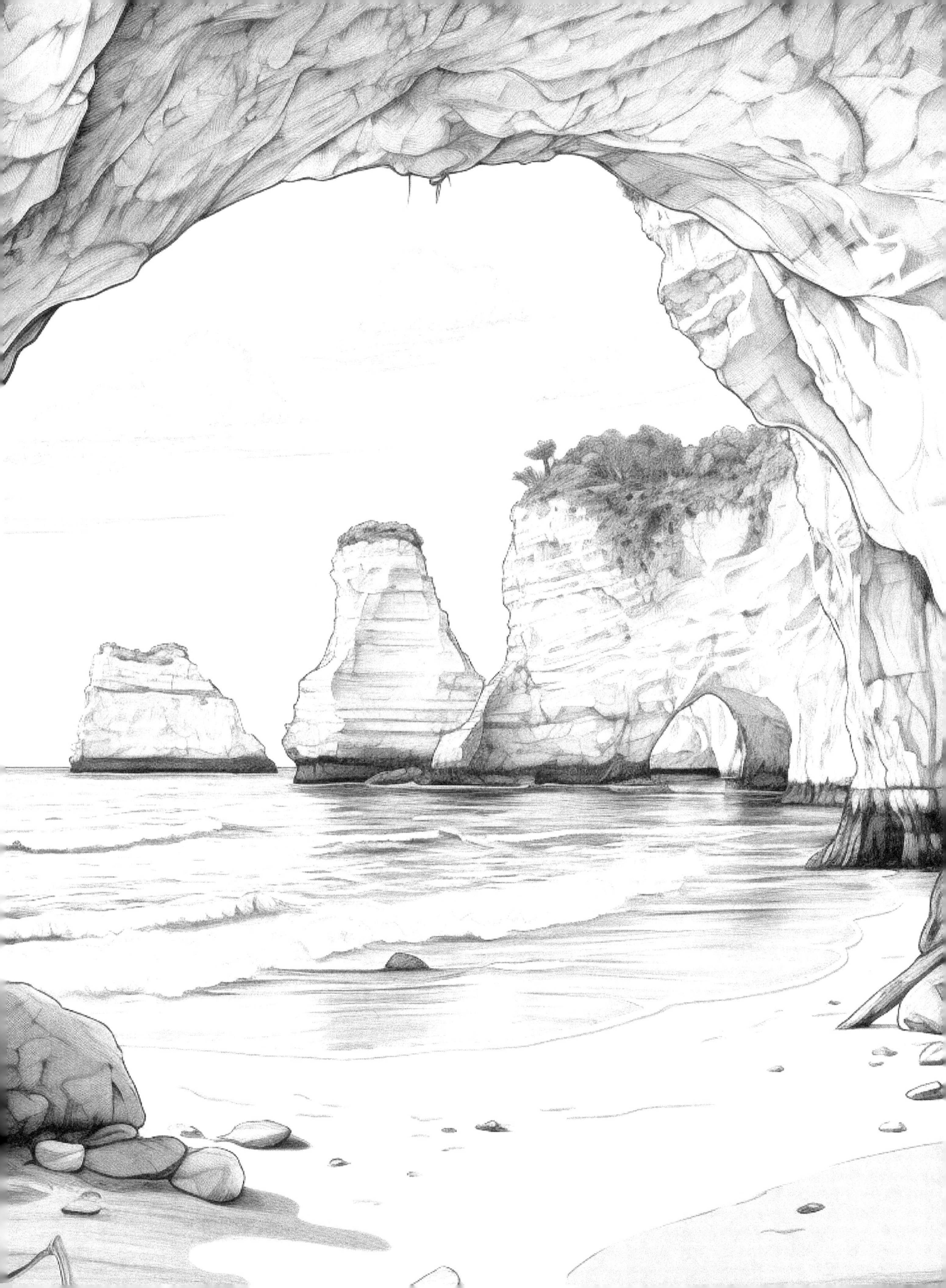

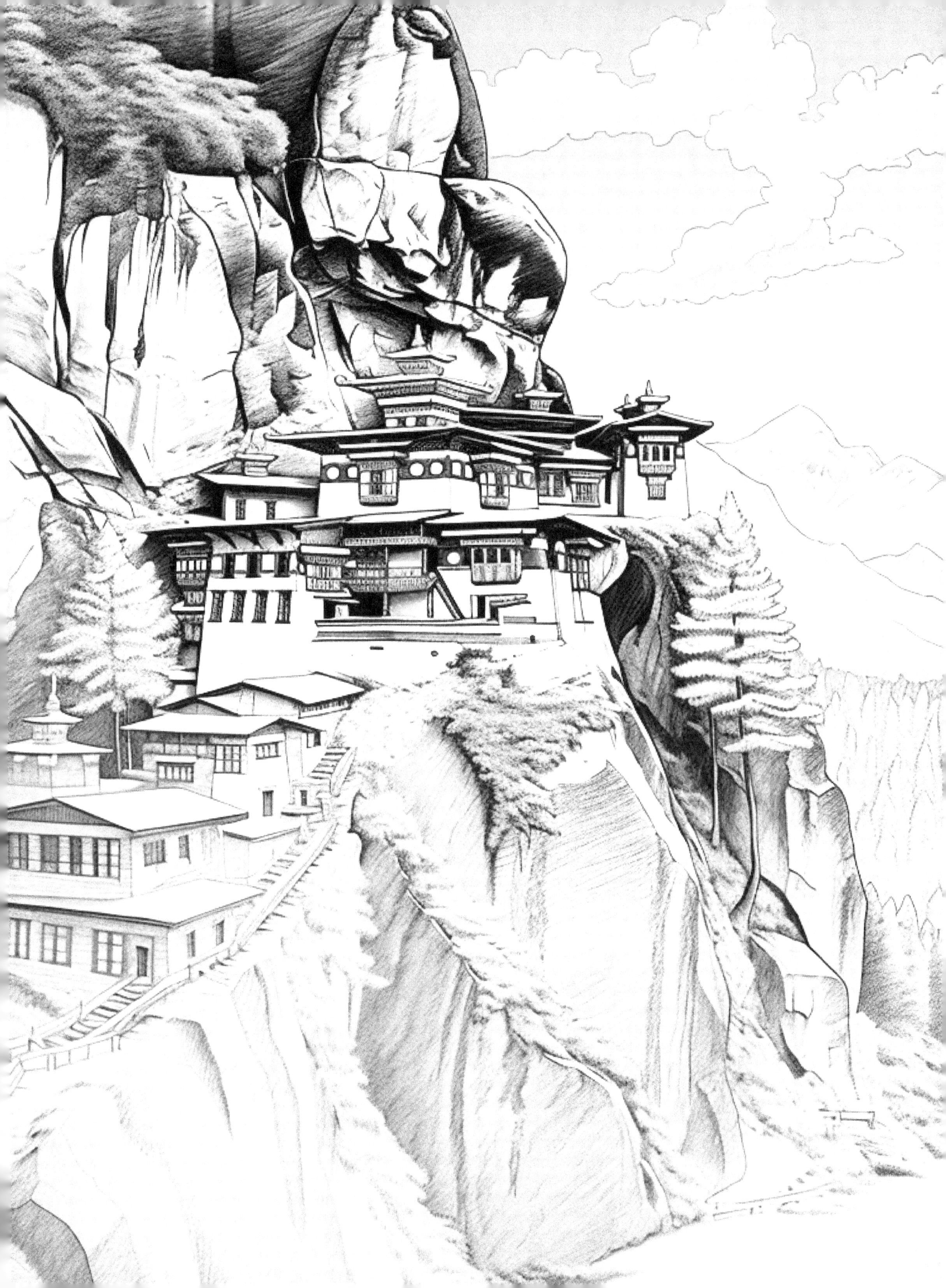

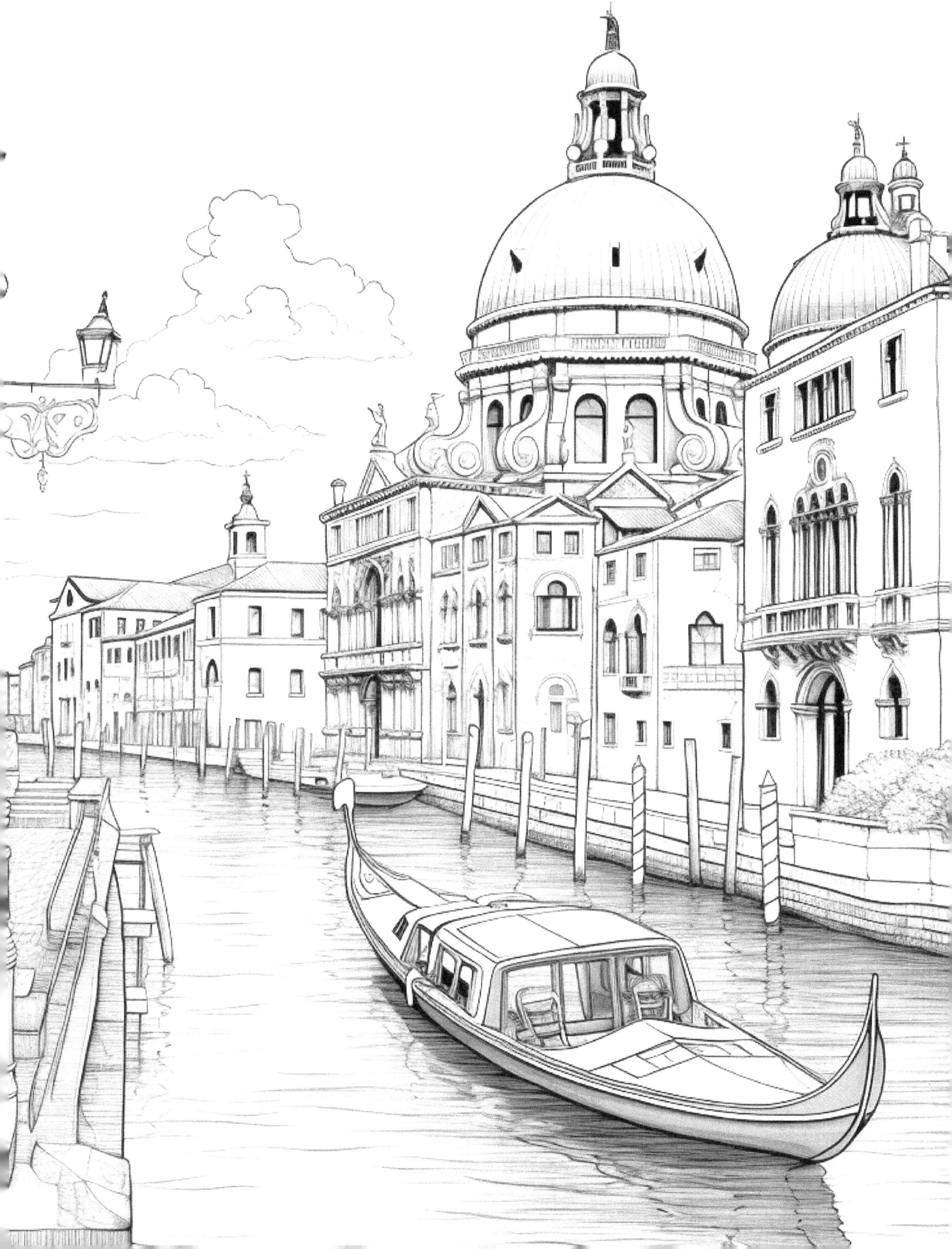

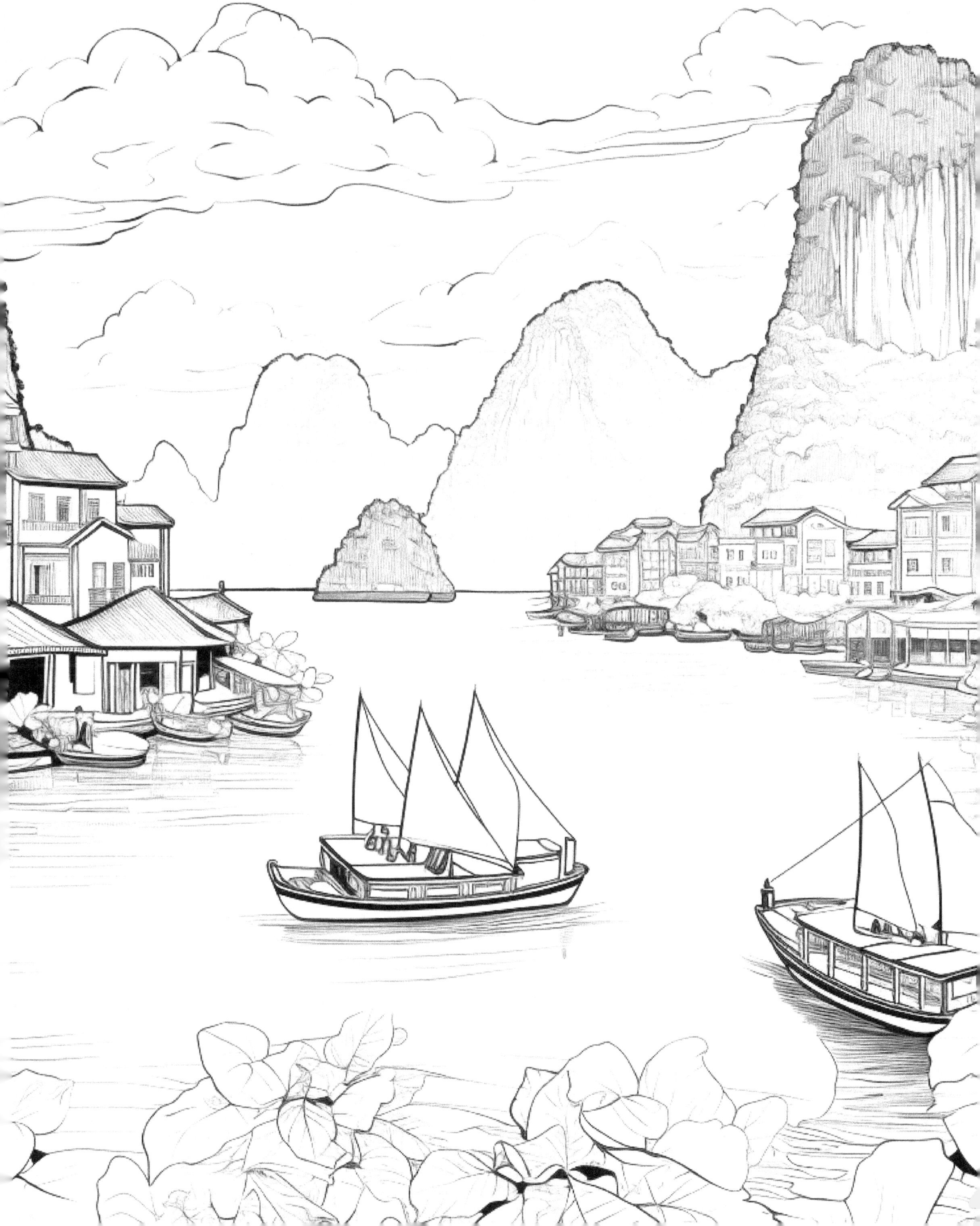

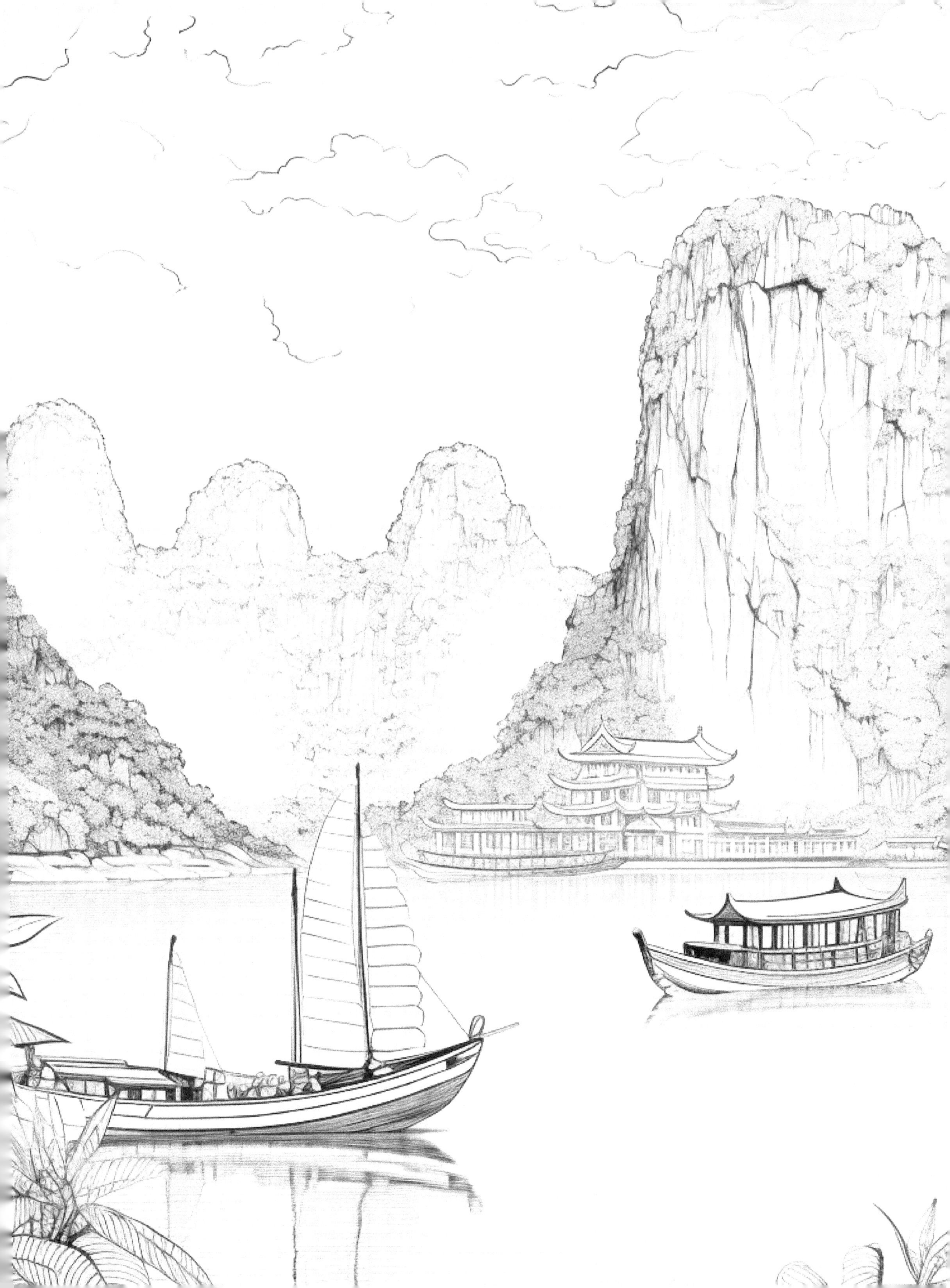

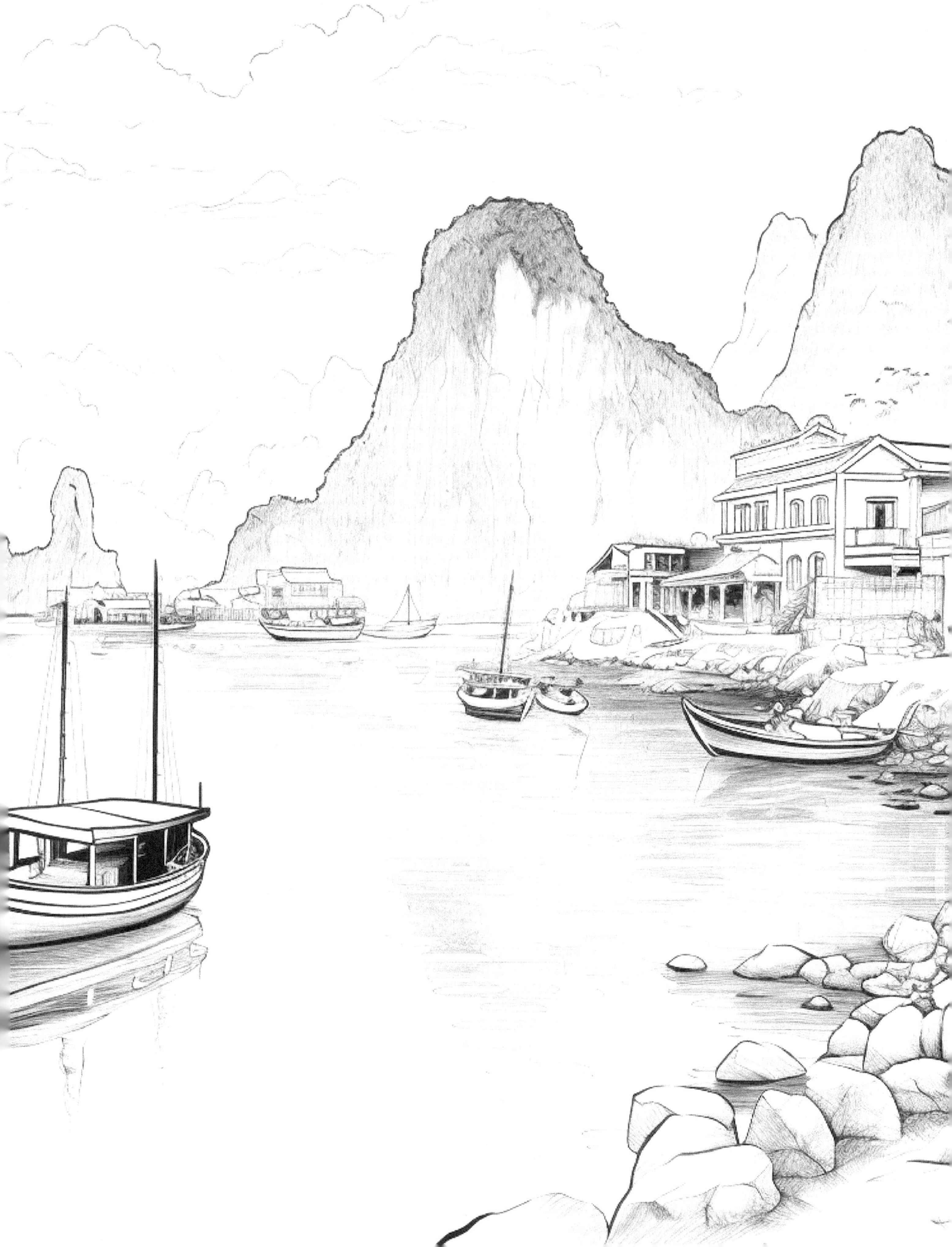

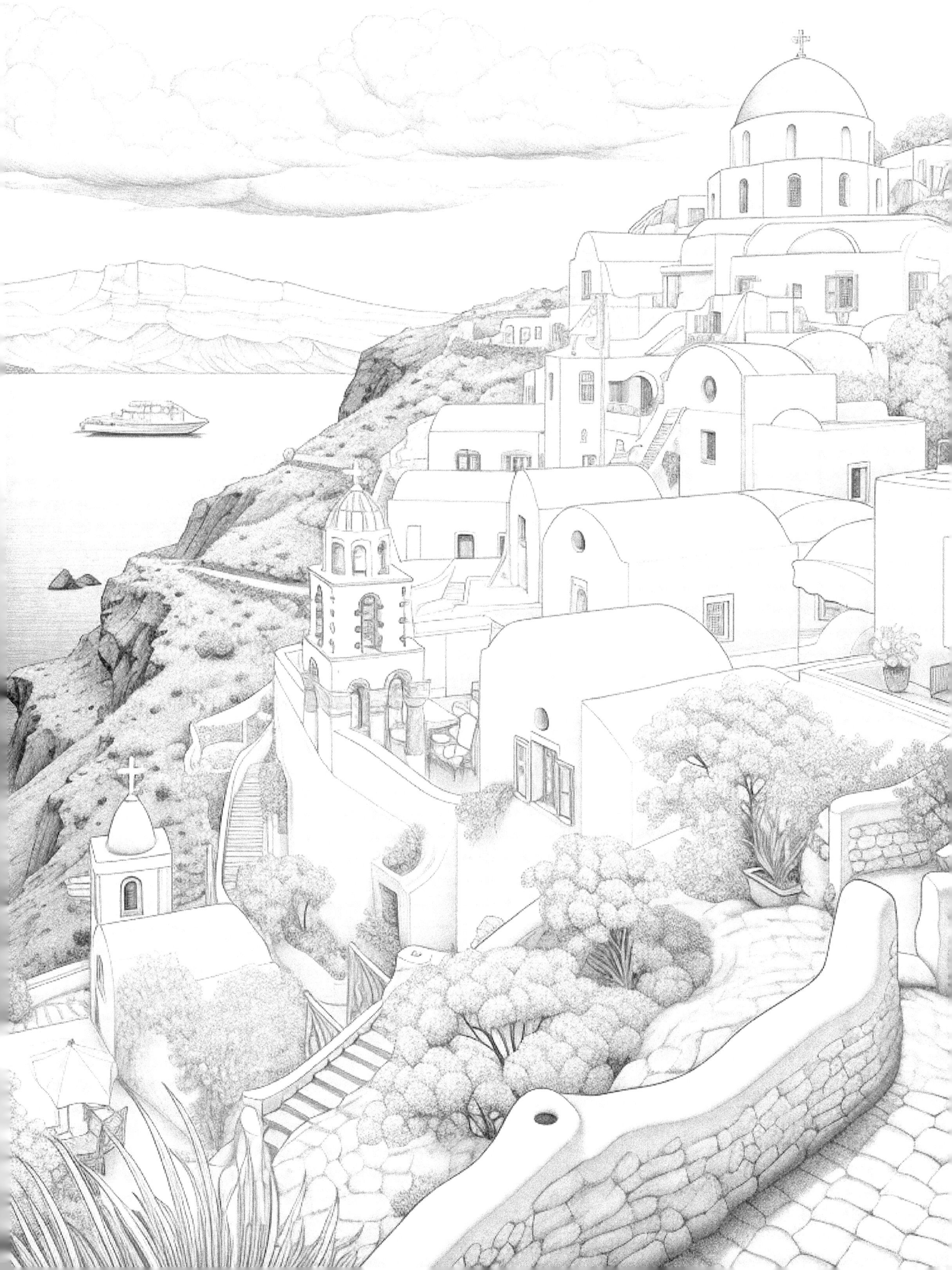

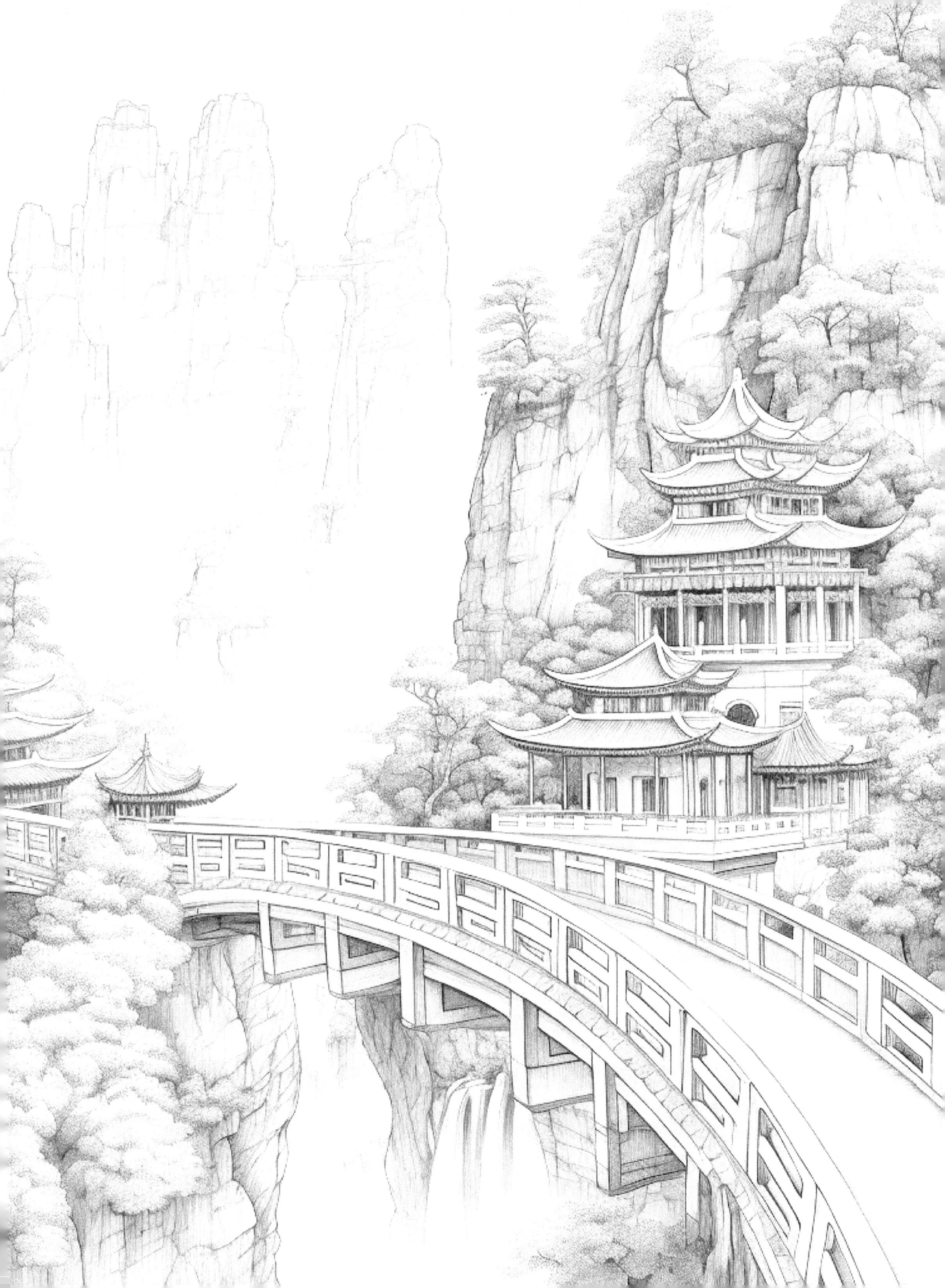

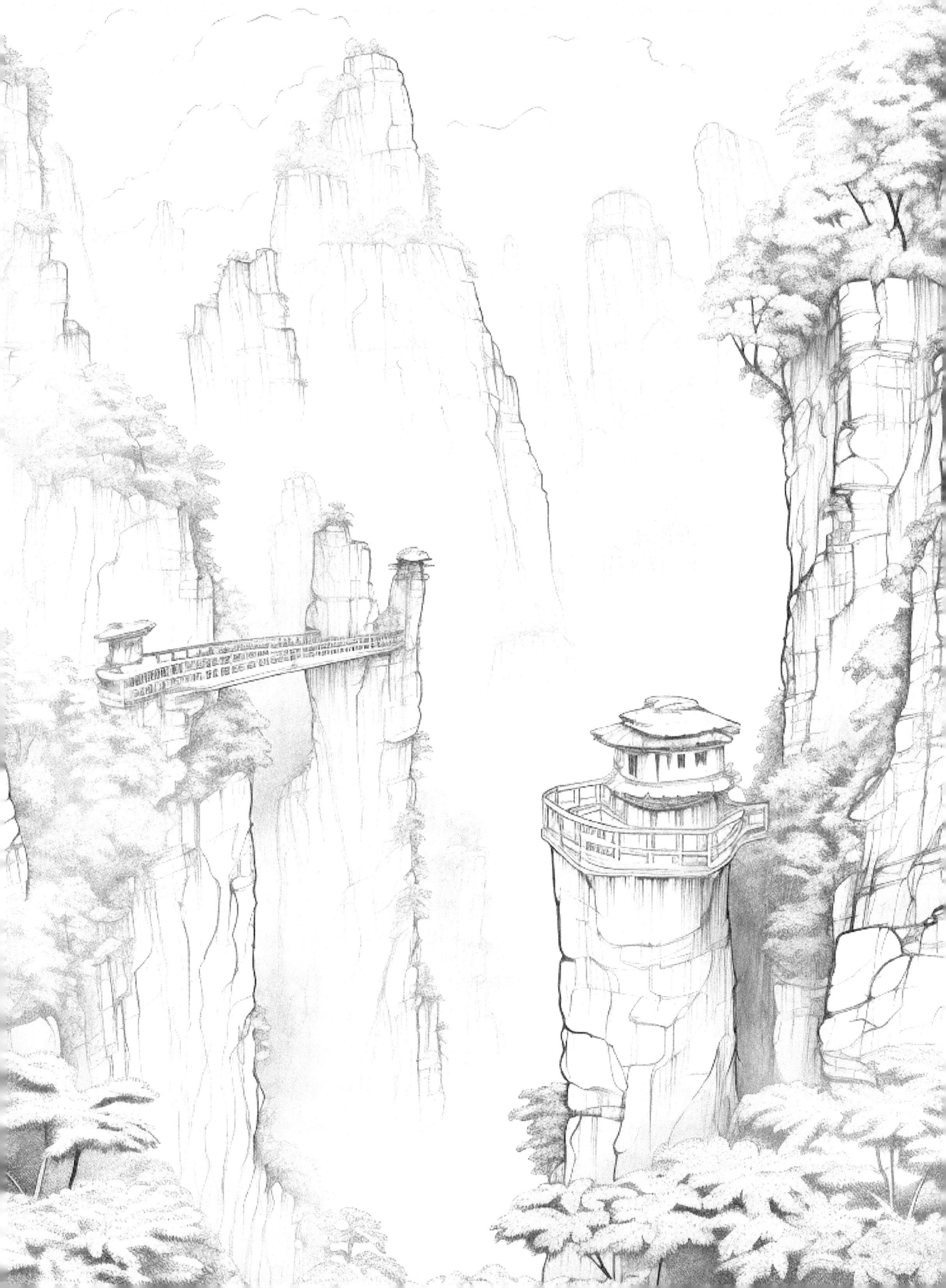

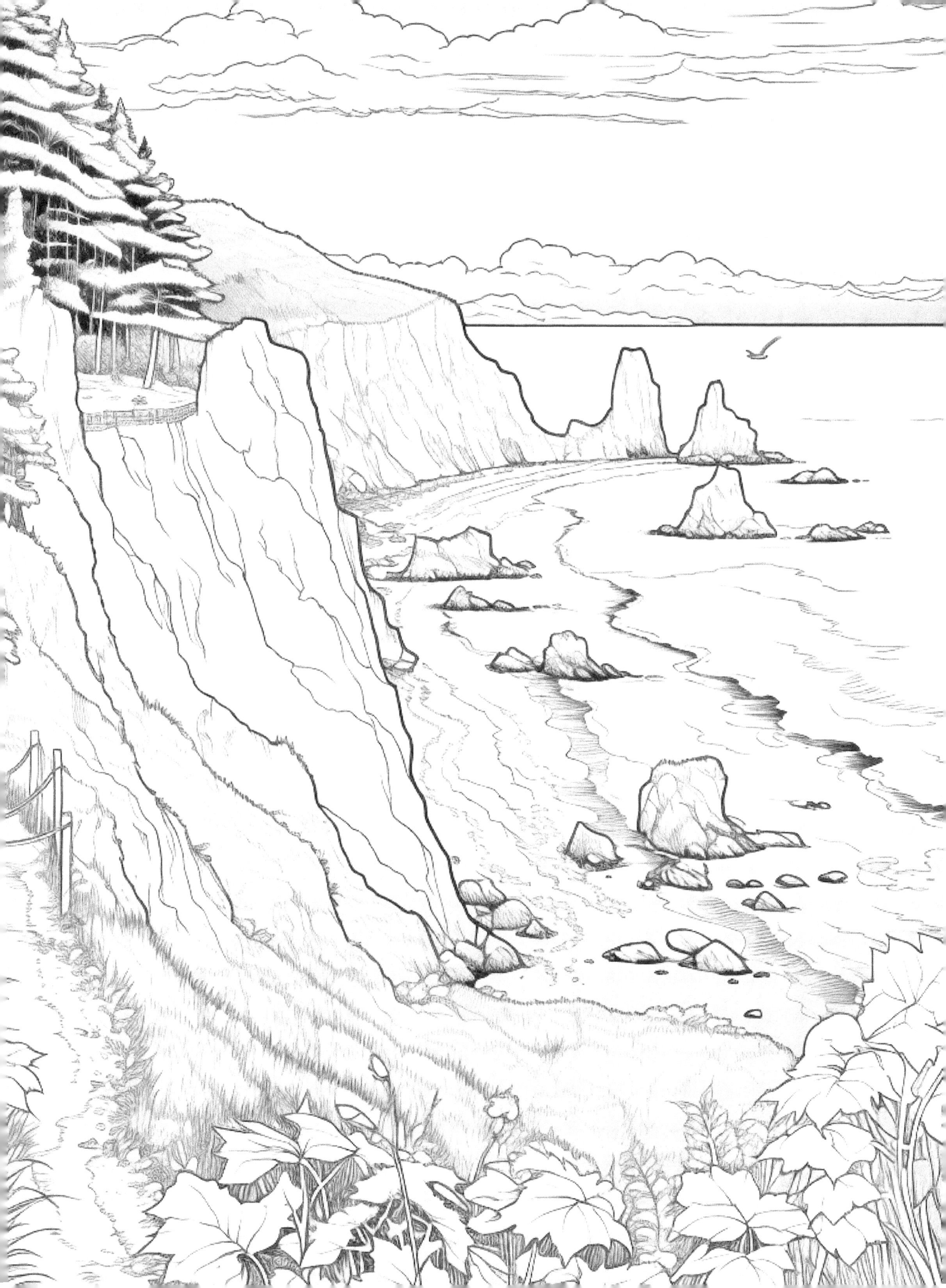

www.ingramcontent.com/pod-product-compliance
Lightning Source LLC
Chambersburg PA
CBHW082143290526
45794CB00008B/3143
9798850839673